Discovering East Lothian

Discovering
East Lothian

IAN AND KATHLEEN WHYTE

JOHN DONALD PUBLISHERS
EDINBURGH

ISBN 0 85976 222 X

Phototypeset by Newtext Composition Ltd., Glasgow.
Printed in Great Britain by Bell & Bain Ltd., Glasgow.

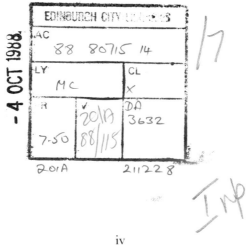

Contents

Maps

Introduction

The main features of East Lothian's landscape have been fashioned by its geology over hundreds of millions of years and much of the detail is the result of the work of ice sheets within the last few tens of thousands of years. The appearance of the countryside today is, however, almost entirely due to the activities of man over the last few thousand years. No part of East Lothian, from the heights of Lammer Law to the rocky islands off North Berwick, has escaped the effects of human activity. As we shall see, most of the area, including the Lammermuir hills, has actually been settled by man at one time or another. The geology of East Lothian, the shaping of its topography, and its natural history are topics which we explore in Chapter 1. Nevertheless, discovering East Lothian largely involves the story of how man used the landscape at different periods and how this has given the area its present-day character. Part of this story concerns the great landowners but much of it is the result of ordinary people shaping around them a working landscape which changed through time, sometimes gradually, sometimes rapidly, leaving behind many traces today.

Much of our story concerns East Lothian from medieval times onwards, especially the period from the seventeeth century to the present. This is not because earlier periods are uninteresting but because much of what happened is beyond recovery as most traces of man's early activities have been obliterated by later generations. Nevertheless, East Lothian has many interesting prehistoric monuments, which we look at in Chapters 3 and 4, and one or two sites from the Dark Ages which are worth a visit.

The modern landscape is a composite one containing features from the Bronze Age onwards although those from recent centuries inevitably predominate. Although there are some fine medieval buildings in the area, a recurring theme in most chapters is the importance of the later eighteenth and nineteenth centuries in the creation of the modern landscape.

1

The Agricultural Revolution changed the face of the county within two or three generations, the fastest and most complete period of change in the area's history (Chapter 5). Much of the countryside which you can see today dates from this period. Seventeeth and early-eighteenth-century English travellers found East Lothian fertile but bleak, impoverished, and unimproved. By the early nineteeth century visitors were astonished at the efficiency of its agriculture and the neat, tidy appearance of its field and farmsteads.

Although East Lothian has an essential unity as an area, a striking feature is the variety of its landscapes though the differences are often subtle. Along the coast the sandy estuaries of the Tyne and Peffer Burn contrast with the cliffs around North Berwick and south of Dunbar. This is very much a holiday coast today and it is easy to forget how important the sea, and coastal transport, was in the life of East Lothian in the past. This is emphasised by the string of small harbours, some merely rocky clefts, others little better than open beaches, which were once thriving centres of fishing and trade (Chapter 10).

Within the lowlands there is a marked contrast between the open coastal plain in the north and the more sheltered valley of the River Tyne. Both areas have a marked appearance of order and efficiency with big, compact farmsteads and large, regular fields. The landscape is often open but well-tended, without the bleakness which you often get with Scottish farmland. Between the fields and farmsteads there is also a fair amount of woodland, a reminder of the high density of estates in this area as much of its encloses the parklands or 'policies' of country houses.

South of the Tyne the countryside becomes more broken and wooded as it rises towards the foothills of the Lammermuirs. The fringes of the hills are less well known than the lowlands, with hidden villages like Garvald and Oldhamstocks nestling in the valleys (Chapter 7). The Lammermuirs themselves are a world of their own. East Lothian is often thought of as a lowland area, but if you stop in one of the lay-bys on the A1 between Haddington and East Linton and look to the south, beyond the whale-backed ridge of Traprain Law you will see the long blue line of the hills. East

Lothian's boundary lies well beyond their crest. The Lammermuirs are not as impressive as other Borders hill areas. They are more distinctive from below that on top, for their summit is a series of plateaus and flat-topped ridges and their very flatness emphasises their lonliness. The lowlands of East Lothian are densely settled but you can walk down some of the streams which drain south to the Leader or the Whiteadder for a whole day and hardly meet a soul.

We have taken as the limits of our area the boundaries of the modern East Lothian district, created in 1975. This may sound arbitrary and you might wonder whether these boundaries define a distinctive region. In fact the modern boundaries reflect divisions which go back to medieval times and perhaps even into prehistory. When the Romans annexed south-east Scotland they found it occupied by a tribe which they named the Votadini whose territory included the modern Lothians and the Berwickshire Merse. Their capital was the great hill-fort on Traprain Law (Chapter 3), suggesting that the core of their territory was East Lothian. By the end of the sixth century A.D. a tribe called the Gododdin held the Lothians and the Lammermuirs had become a boundary between them and the expanding Anglian kingdom of Bernicia which eventually absorbed them.

During the period of Anglian domination the activities of the mysterious and shadowy Saint Baldred are associated with East Lothian. A later chronicle claims that he ministered to the inhabitants of the country between the Esk and Lammermuir. In this context 'Lammermuir' seems to have meant the area where the hills come down to the sea between Innerwick and Cockburnspath. Thus by the early-Christian period the limits of modern East Lothian had been defined. The Lammermuirs made an obvious barrier to the south. The Esk was the main natural boundary across the lowlands east of Edinburgh. The Dunglass Burn, at the narrowest part of the coastal route from the Merse into Lothian, was also a clear divide. It was along these boundaries that the medieval constabulary, and later the sheriffdom, centred on Haddington grew up although a small area east of the Esk became incorporated into Midlothian. The local government re-organisation of the mid-1970s pushed the district boundary west of Esk and a little beyond, enabling us to

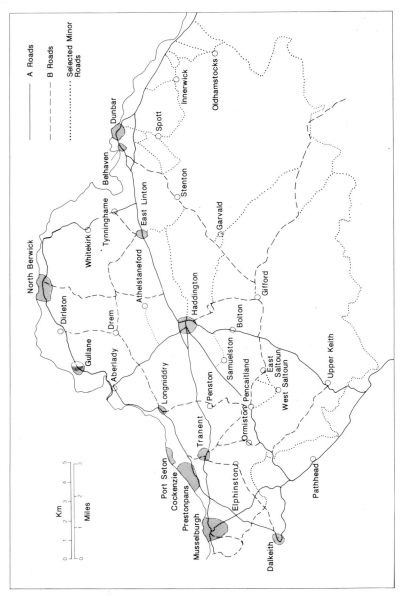

Map 1. East Lothian – Location Map

include Musselburgh within the scope of our book.

This is a book for everyone who is interested in East Lothian, both residents and visitors, but it is not a place-by-place guidebook. We have taken a series of themes and developed them in separate chapters which cover the county as a whole. We have done this because we believe that to really discover an area you need to consider it as a whole in order to appreciate the relationships of the various places within it. Our aim is to indicate some of the most interesting things to see but to set them within a wider context so that you can appreciate why they are there and why they are worth visiting. The chapters cover obvious features like castles, country houses and churches, but also less obvious ones like old roads, farmsteads and industrial sites. The gazetteer at the end of the book, with its cross references to the text, along with the maps, will help to show you what to see in any place. Within the text we have given frequent map references to places that we think are worth visiting. These references relate to the National Grid which is marked, and explained, on Ordnance Survey maps. Some topics are just touched on incidentally, such as the history of the area's landed families, because this book focuses on what you can actually see and discover for yourself in the landscape rather than on what you can glean in libraries from old parish and family histories.

While a car may be necessary to get you to East Lothian, a good way to explore the area is on foot or by bicycle. If you are unfamiliar with the area, Map 1 will give you your bearings. For exploring the area properly we recommend more detailed maps. The Ordnance Survey Landranger series, sheets 66 and 67, at a scale of 1:50,000, or two centimetres to one kilometre, is ideal for getting around by car and for finding interesting stopping places. The Pathfinder series, at a scale of 1:25,000, or four centimetres to one kilometre, is more detailed and more useful if you are walking or cycling. Remember that much of the county is farmland and that there are no rights of way across the fields unless a footpath is signposted. The dense network of minor roads and farm tracks will take you almost anywhere without fear of trespass but you should ask permission before cutting across fields. Our description of any site in this book is no guarantee of a right of access. If you are walking in the Lammermuirs, access is fairly open but remember that this area is shot over for grouse and avoid the grouse-shooting season from the 12th August. The Lammermuirs are easy hill-walking country but the weather can turn nasty on the summits. Waterproof clothing and stout footwear should be worn if you are venturing far from a road.

In preparing this book we would like to acknowledge the help of Belhaven Breweries, the East Lothian Tourist Board, Haddington Public Library, the tourist information office at Dunbar, and the Scottish Mining Museum. We are particularly grateful to Dr. John Shaw of the Royal Museum of Scotland for help and advice, and to Claire Jarvis and Peter Mingins for drawing the maps.

CHAPTER 1
Nature's Landscape

Although most of this book is about the history of East Lothian and how you can discover it for yourself in the landscape, it is important to know a little about how the landscape has evolved under the influence of nature. The geology of East Lothian has shaped the scenery and this in turn has affected man. To appreciate how East Lothian's scenery has been formed it is necessary to understand a little of its geology. By geology we mean both the solid rocks which form the bones of the country and the mantle of superficial deposits – sands, gravel silts and clays – which covers them like a skin.

Rocks and Scenery

The best vantage point from which to see how geology has shaped East Lothian's scenery is the Hopetoun Monument (501764) on the summit of the Garleton Hills north of Haddington. From there on a clear day you can see the main elements of the area's geology. Figures 1 and 2 will help you to fit the following outline into place. The long blue line of the Lammermuirs to the south marks the most siginificant geological boundary in the area; between the ancient hard rocks of the Southern Uplands and the softer, younger sediments forming the plain around you. This plain is part of the Central Lowlands of Scotland, a great rift valley produced by major earth movements between two huge fractures or 'faults' in the earth's crust. The steep northward face of the Lammermuirs marks the line of one of these faults. Subsidence of the land to the north of it and uplift to the south has brought old hard rocks up against younger, softer ones, forming a prominent step in the landscape.

The Lammermuirs are mainly formed of rocks called greywackes (hardened sandstone) and shales which were laid down as sand and mud in a trough below the ocean during the Ordovician and Silurian periods some 530-440 million years

7

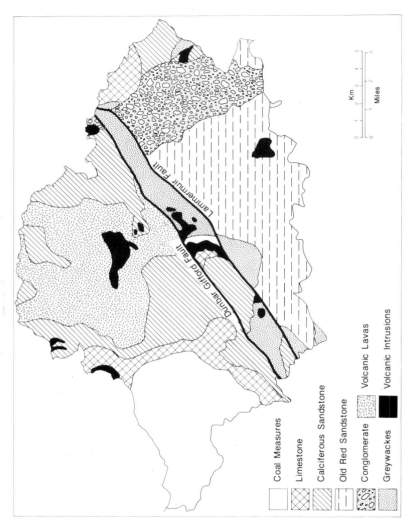

Map 2. Geology

ago. These deposits were gradually compressed and hardened into rock, then lifted up, tightly folded and further hardened under pressure until they formed a block of upstanding hill country. Over millennia the effects of wind and weather, and the action of streams in eroding this ancient range, produced valleys in which debris washed down from the hills was deposited and in turn eventually hardened into rock. Modern valleys like Lauderdale on the southern side of the Lammermuirs were ancient valleys which have been re-cut in more recent geological times by rivers which have removed this infilling of rock. In the east of the Lammermuirs there is a belt of rock known as conglomerate – a mixture of stones and pebbles in a sandy matrix – still filling an ancient valley which has yet to be dug out by a modern river. Because this conglomerate has proved to be so resistant to erosion, it now forms quite upstanding country above the ancient infilled valley.

The grewackes and shales of the Lammermuirs were worn away over a long period before new earth movements led to parts of them being submerged by the sea where new rocks were laid down on top of them. There is thus a big chronological gap between the folded and buckled greywackes whose upper strata have been stripped off, and the rocks which were laid down immediately on top of them on the bed of the new ocean. This major break in the strata is marked in rock sections along the coastline south of Dunbar by a contrast between the tightly-folded older rocks below and the more horizontally bedded ones above which were deposited on top of their worn edges. Because of this break in the geological record and the contrasting orientation of the beds of rock this feature is known as an 'unconformity'. This area is one of the classic localities whose evidence allowed the general principles of the fledgling science of geology to be established in the nineteenth century by pioneers like Hutton and Playfair. The best-known site showing this unconformity is at Siccar Point (812709), just inside Berwickshire, but other examples can be seen along the seashore in this area.

To the north of the Lammermuirs much of the plain is formed from sediments – sandstones, limestones and coal measures – which accumulated in lakes, lagoons and shallow seas 400-350 million years ago. There are also areas of volcanic rocks, including the Garleton Hills on which you are standing. Although the lowlands of East Lothian are composed of such a variety of rocks, they do not differ very markedly in their tendancy to erode, and the resulting landscape is a gently undulating plain. One of the most distinctive of these rocks is the bright Old Red Sandstone which occurs in a belt along the edge of the Lammermuirs from Dunbar through Stenton. It provides the warm red building stone from which much of Dunbar is built and gives the same distinct colouring to the soils in the area. Younger than the Old Red Sandstone, other, paler sandstones continue upwards into the strata of the Carboniferous period which includes the coal measures as well as limestones and shales.

The coal measures occur in the west of the county in a shallow basin fringed with limestones which outcrop on the coast near Aberlady and contain a wide range of fossils. The coal measures run back from the sea inland below Tranent and fade out south of Ormiston. At various places within this great saucer seams of coal reached the surface and were easily mined in the past (Chapter 9). They also outcrop along the coast where they have been worked from medieval times. The thickest coal seams are towards the centre of the basin, and although they occur at the surface, in places much of the coal lies very deep, and it has only been possible to reach these seams with relatively modern mining technology. This coal basin has been important to East Lothian by providing it with the basis for industrial developoment from the sixteenth century onwards (Chapter 9). South of Dunbar a smaller basin of Carboniferous rock occurs with some thin seams of coal and, as at Aberlady, the outcrops of limestones along the coast at Barns Ness (724773) provide a good hunting ground for fossils, particularly corals.

Much of the middle of the county from North Berwick to Haddington is made up of volcanic rocks. These date from a period of eruptions during Carboniferous times. The entire area must have been a real hell's kitchen when all the volcanoes were in eruption. Some rocks in this area have been formed from lavas which were thrown out at the surface. Others are the solidified remains of molten material which seeped between cracks in the sedimentary rocks well below ground level and have been brought to light by the erosion of the rocks on top of them. Some of the volcanic rocks form prominent landscape features, such as the Garleton Hills, Traprain Law (582748), North Berwick Law (556843), and the islands of Fidra, Craigleith and the Bass Rock offshore from North Berwick. Others, mainly lava flows, spread out over the countryside without creating distinctive landforms.

Traprain Law was formed from lava which was squeezed in between layers of other rocks far below the surface and bulged up into a dome. Eventually this was exposed when the overlying sediments were stripped away. The Garleton Hills were formed in a similar manner. The Bass Rock and North Berwick Law are plugs of lava which have been solidified in the vents of former volcanoes whose cones have been totally worn away. The country north of the Garleton Hills was originally a lava plain over which molten material poured out quietly from a number of small openings, spreading out and hardening to form basalt. This rock gives buildings in North Berwick and Haddington a darker colour than those in Dunbar. Along the coast near North Berwick and Dunbar are the remains of a number of small volcanoes which help to make this stretch of coastline so varied and attractive. Plugs of lava which hardened in the vents of these volcanoes have been left as small rocky outcrops; along the foreshore at Dunbar there are more than twenty, some very small, others nearly a kilometre in diameter. The cliffs on which Dunbar Castle stands and the rocky stacks offshore are examples of these volcanic necks and you can buy a booklet in Dunbar which describes these in detail as part of an attractive coastal walk.

The Legacy of the Ice Age

The broad features of East Lothian's scenery were already in existence two million years ago but much of the fine detail of topography which we can see today is due to the effects of the ice age. At its maximum extent ice completely covered the area to a depth of several hundred metres, grinding away at the rocks at its base, removing the debris and modifying the

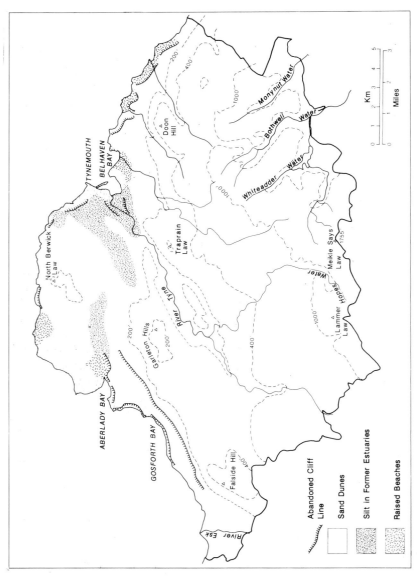

Map 3. Surface Features

landscape as it went. The ice moved out from the Highlands and swept eastwards across the county. This eastward movement, and the tremendous power of the ice to shape the landscape, is shown by the shape of hills like Traprain Law and North Berwick Law. Their western ends, facing the direction from which the ice came, are steep and craggy where the ice has scoured them, but their eastern sides, in the lee of the ice-flow and protected by the bulk of the hills, form longer, gently-sloping tails.

At the base of the ice fragments were plucked and worn away from the bedrock and carried along to be deposited as an unsorted mixture of debris, known as boulder clay or 'till', containing everything from small stones to huge boulders set in a clayey matrix. This till is plastered over the lowlands to a depth of 5-10m in most places, smoothing the contours of the land surface. Sometimes, however, till finds deeper hollows and valleys which existed before the ice advanced. In places the till has been sculptured by the ice into low ridges which run east-west, parallel to the direction of ice flow. The till at any locality is mostly derived from local rocks and tends to take on their colouring but it also contains some far-travelled stones and boulders, or 'erratics', some of which have been carried from as far away as the Highlands. One erratic at Kidlaw (509645), a huge block of limestone, is over half a kilometre long and even has a quarry in it! Geologists originally thought that it was a natural outcrop of rock until they found that glacial till lay underneath it.

As the climate began to warm up and the ice sheet started to melt, some 15,000 years ago, the Lammermuirs began to emerge but the lowlands to the north were still buried by ice. Water ran down the northern face of the hills and was trapped against the edge of the ice, as was meltwater trickling off the ice sheet itself. This water flowed eastwards between the hills and the ice sheet which sloped downwards in this direction. The meltwater cut a series of channels into the northern foothills of the Lammermuirs, some running across the slope, others dropping straight down, showing where the water found an escape route deeper into the ice. As the ice surface gradually melted downwards, these channels were cut at lower and lower levels along the fringes of the Lammermuirs and eventually, at a late stage in the break-up of the ice, along the northern edge of the Garleton Hills too.

Some of these channels appear today as terraces on the hillside because when they were originally cut, ice formed one side of the trough. Other channels are proper valleys, some of them 60m deep. This complex series of channels, running from east of Gifford round the edge of the hills to well south of Dunbar, gives the northern fringes of the Lammermuirs much of their variety. Some meltwater channels contain present-day steams which are clearly far too small to have cut them while others are entirely dry. One of the most impressive is the channel which cuts the hill of Deuchrie Dod off from the rest of the Lammermuirs. It runs from the farm of Deuchrie (623714) for over a kilometre and a half north-eastwards and, although marshy in places, has no modern stream flowing through it. The meltwaters which cut these channels carried large quantities of sand and gravel and dropped them at the mouths of the channels in large spreading fans. A belt of these sands and gravels occurs around the edge of the Lammermuirs and along the coast south of Dunbar where it provides light, dry, easily-worked soils which are ideal for growing potatoes.

The ice sheets affected the pattern of the streams throughout the county by burying the old pre-glacial valleys with deposits of till. After the ice retreated, streams sometimes had to cut new valleys because their old ones were so thoroughly blocked. This is the case with the River Tyne below Haddington. It originally flowed further to the north; boreholes have discovered a wide buried channel, the old Tyne valley, below Beanston (549763). The river was unable to re-excavate this section of its valley and instead cut a new gorge through solid basalt at Hailes (574759). Glacial meltwaters sometimes carved new ready-made valleys though; the River Tyne between Ormiston and Pencaitland flows through a valley which is far too large for the diminuitive stream – 'river' is really only a courtesy title at this point. The valley was cut by a powerful flow of meltwater which came from the west through a gap (now dry) near Borthwick.

North Berwick Law: one of East Lothian's most spectacular volcanic hills, crowned by the ramparts of an Iron Age fort, and a magnificent viewpoint.

After the Ice

At the end of the ice age, between about 15,000 and 10,000 years ago, the sea was higher relative to the land than at present. This was due to vast quantities of water being released from melting ice sheets at a time when the land, which had been pushed down by the weight of the ice, had not begun to recover. These high late-glacial seas cut a series of cliffs and platforms which are now far inland, up to 35m above present sea level (Figure 2). Between Port Seton and Longniddry you can trace this abandoned shoreline, which is about a kilometre inland, as a marked step in the landscape. The railway runs along the top of it between Longniddry and Drem. At the same time the sea flooded the valley of the Peffer Burn east of Aberlady, reaching through to the coast at Tyninghame and cutting off the area around North Berwick and Dirleton from the rest of East Lothian. The mudflats in this estuary were later to form some of the richest soils in the county.

As sea level gradually fell with the recovery of the land from the weight of the ice, lower cliff lines were cut but these are not

15

as prominent as the highest level mentioned above. After the end of the ice age, from about 7000 to 5000 years ago, sea level was higher again – long enough for waves to cut a platform and cliffs in solid rock at about 8m above present sea level. This cliffline, much closer to the sea than the late-glacial one, is prominent around North Berwick and at Dunbar where much of the town is built on the abandoned beach. At Aberlady you drop down over the old cliff where the road at the east end of the village turns sharply towards the sea.

As the climate became warmer with the retreat of the ice, a vegetation cover began to clothe the bare stony landscape. At first this was only sparse tundra like the present Arctic, but slowly scrub and then trees became established, mainly hardy pine and birch. As the climate improved, more warmth-loving trees like oak and elm spread into the lowlands with alder in the wetter areas until a cover of deciduous woodland extended over virtually the entire county except for exposed coastal locations, some marshy hollows and the highest parts of the Lammermuirs.

Soils, Climate and Farming

The combination of different types of bedrock and drift, along with variations in the vegetation cover, produced East Lothian's soils. Over much of the lowlands these have developed on till, forming rich, deep clays which are high in nutrients and are well suited to arable farming. The dry climate means that waterlogging is rarely a problem for farmers while the gentle slopes seldom impede agricultural machinery. In areas where meltwater streams spread out fans of sand and gravel, or on raised beach deposits, the soils are lighter and warmer and are well suited to horticulture and potato-growing. There is an important belt of horticulture along the coast around Longniddry on top of the late-glacial raised beaches, while large quantities of potatoes are grown on the sands and gravels south of Dunbar.

The East Lothian plain is one of the largest areas of high-quality farmland in Scotland, benefiting from deep, fertile soils and a dry climate. The area receives under 30″ of rain a year

The Bass Rock, showing part of the gannet colony on the cliffs and slopes above and to the right of the lighthouse.

on average while the country north of a line between Longniddry and Dunbar has under 25″. The rainfall does not always come at the right season; springs and summers can be too dry and irrigation is needed for some crops, while there is often more rain at harvest time than farmers would wish. Spring can be made cooler by haar, fog rolling in off the North Sea which blankets the coast and sometimes the entire county in a cold, clammy grasp.

Agriculture in the lowlands today is mainly intensive arable farming with livestock as an important subsidiary element. As you move south and begin to climb into the foothills of the Lammermuirs, climate and soil conditions become less favourable. With increasing altitude temperatures and the amount of sunshine fall, while cloudiness, rainfall and windiness increase. This is reflected by a gradual change in farming with crops becoming less important and livestock taking over as the mainstay of the farmer's livelihood. The Lammermuirs themselves are sheep-farming country. Most of the hill farms have small areas of improved *in-bye* land on which they can grow some oats or at least hay but this is purely for feeding to their flocks. The hills themselves are good sheep pasture compared with many parts of the Scottish uplands; numbers of sheep are higher here because the drier climate provides better-quality grazing and helps cut down the pests and parasites which flourish in more waterlogged conditions. Although East Lothian's scenery has been shaped by its geology, the actual landscape is largely man-made. The forest cover which spread over virtually the whole area, including the Lammermuirs, after the retreat of the ice sheets has been completely removed. As we shall see (Chapter 3), there is evidence of a shortage of timber as early as the Iron Age. The woodland which you see today is the result of deliberate planting from the late seventeenth century onwards (Chapter 5), not a survival from the primeval wildwood. The heather moors and acid grasslands of the Lammermuirs are as artificial as the cultivated lowlands. In the uplands woodland clearance, bad grazing management and over-cultivation of the fragile hill soils in prehistoric and medieval times have caused the widespread erosion and impoverishment of the original woodland soils. Only a thin, acid layer has been left to support the present vegetation cover which is artificially maintained by heather burning and grazing. In the lowlands cultivation over thousands of years has totally altered the original soils, and deep ploughing since the eighteenth century has removed many traces of man's early activities. Even the coast has been modified by human activity. Large areas between Musselburgh and Prestonpans have been reclaimed while the silting up of estuaries like the Esk and the Peffer Burn at Aberlady may be in part the result of the erosion of soil from the agricultural land.

Birdlife

Space does not permit us to look at the natural history of East Lothian in detail, but for visitors to the area one aspect, the birdlife, often proves particularly interesting. Some of the most rewarding sites for birdwatching are around the coast, especially from Aberlady Bay to Dunbar. Aberlady Bay (4680) is a nature reserve but access to it, along the rocky south shore by Kilspindie or the sandy north shore towards Gullane Point, is unrestricted. The sandbanks and mudflats of the bay provide food and refuge for a variety of estuary birds. In winter flocks of up to about 2,500 Pink-footed Geese can be seen, as can smaller numbers of Whooper Swans, Eiders, Wigeon and Sheld Duck as well as large numbers of waders including Dunlins, Turnstones and Oystercatchers. The more exposed Gullane Bay (4783), just to the west, is noted for sea ducks. In winter these may include up to 1,000 Eiders, 2,500 Scoters and smaller flocks of Velvet Scoters.

The rocky island of Fidra (513869) can be visited by boat from North Berwick in summer. It has a tern colony on the low central part of the island with Common and sometimes Roseate terns breeding. Fulmars, Shags and Kittiwakes are also common. The small rock called the Lamb (535867) has a colony of Cormorants.

The Tyne estuary (6379) provides a similar habitat to Aberlady Bay. The northern side of the estuary forms part of the Tyninghame estate but access to the south shore can be obtained from West Barns and Dunbar where there are car parks. On the saltmarsh and more stony areas Skylarks, Meadow Pipits, Linnets and Pied Wagtails are common. Waders include Oystercatchers, Redshank, Ringed and Grey Plovers, Knots and Bar-tailed Godwits. In autumn Sandwich, Arctic and Common terns can be seen while in winter the bay provides a refuge for wildfowl including Whooper Swans, Mallard, Wigeon, Teal, Eider, Sheld Duck, Red-breasted Merganser and Goosander. As with Aberlady Bay a wide range of less common species can be seen on migration.

East Lothian's biggest attraction for the birdwatcher is the Bass Rock (602874) with its 11,000 breeding pairs of gannets. Indeed, the gannet takes its Latin name, Sula Bassana, from the island. Gannets are large white seabirds with black wingtips, a rather angry-looking expression and a wingspan of over 5½ feet. Seen from the cliffs of Tantallon in summer, this impressively rocky island seems to be surrounded by a snowstorm of them. They wheel around in search of fish and plummet into the sea in a vertical dive, sometimes to depths of fifty feet or more. Their skulls are specially strengthened to withstand the tremendous impact of hitting the water. A friend of ours, scuba diving off the island, once found a dead gannet which had mistaken a plank for something edible and had bored its way through a thick layer of oak. He then considered what impression a short-sighted gannet might make on his skull and beat a hasty retreat!

The Bass Rock and its gannets, or solan geese as they were once called, were, from the sixteenth century at least, a tourist attraction for visitors travelling from Berwick to Edinburgh. The birds also formed a regular source of food for local residents. When the castle on the Bass Rock was in use the garrison is said to have subsisted largely on a diet of gannet, as perhaps did St. Baldred, the hermit, who supposedly had his cell on the island many centuries before. Only young birds were taken and sold. They were captured by lowering men on ropes from the clifftops. They caught and killed the young birds with hooks and threw them down to waiting boatmen. The cooked birds tasked, as you might imagine, rather fishy; supposedly a gourmet dish but definitely not to everyone's taste! John Taylor, the Water Poet, passing this way in the early seventeenth century, thought young gannet 'a most delicate fowle' but admitted that it went down best when followed quickly but two or three glasses of sherry or canary sack!

Today trips round the Bass Rock can be made from North Berwick in summer and landings can sometimes be arranged. The noise, as well as the smell, can be overpowering but the nesting birds on the more gentle sloping grassy areas towards the summit of the island can be approached quite closely. Where there is enough space they build their large nests only about three feet apart. Despite their close spacing they are aggressive, perennially engaged in trying to steal nest material from their neighbours; hence the noise! Gannets do not have brood patches and they incubate their single egg by keeping it warm beneath their webbed feet. This practice gave rise to the story that their old name, Solan Goose, was derived from 'sole-on' goose!

In winter adult birds disperse around British waters but younger adults may venture as far as West Africa or the Mediterranean. Unlike many species of seabird which have been declining in numbers in recent years, the gannets of the

Traprain Law, capital of the late Bronze Age tribe known to the
Romans as the Votadini, who occupied much of the Lothians and
Berwickshire.

Bass Rock seem to be thriving following a severe decline in the
middle of the last century. By 1850 there were only around
3,500 pairs breeding on the rock and the increase since then
has probably been due to the ending of the practice of taking
them for food. Although the gannets are the Bass Rock's main
attraction for the birdwatcher, other species, including
Fulmars, Kittiwakes, Cormorants, Shags, Herring Gulls,
Greater and Lessed Black-Backed Gulls, Razorbills, Guillemots
and Puffins, also breed on the island.

The John Muir Country Park

East Lothian's coasts have been less affected by man than
most parts of the county and one of the best places to study
wildlife is the John Muir Country Park which extends from
Dunbar Castle westwards to Ravensheugh Sands. There are car
parks at the Castle and at West Barns. The park covers an area
of 1667 acres with a variety of habitats including dunes,
saltmarshes, cliffs, and beaches. There is a nature trail along
the coast with a descriptive guide to the geology, botany,
birdlife and scenery. The geology of the volcanic necks along
the coast at Dunbar is extremely interesting and some 400
plant species have been identified within the park. The range
of shore and estuary birds which can be seen at most seasons is
considerable. The park is named after John Muir, who was
born in Dunbar in 1838 and emigrated with his parents to
America at the age of eleven. He was a pioneer conservationist

21

and was instrumental in having America's first National parks established. He is better known in America than in his native country but the park, the first of its kind in Scotland, is a fitting monument to his work. His birthplace at 126-128 High Street, Dunbar, has been converted into a museum.

CHAPTER 2

Patterns of Belief

Since his earliest appearance in East Lothian man has had some
kind of religious beliefs and these appear in the landscape in a
variety of ways. When we think of religion in this country we
automatically think of Christian worship but there are signs in
the landscape of organised beliefs and rituals from thousands
of years before the arrival of Christianity. This chapter looks at
these pre-Christian features and then traces the history of the
Christian faith in East Lothian through its visible elements,
from Dark Age crosses to eighteenth-century tombstones.

Circles and Standing Stones: Prehistoric Religion

East Lothian does not have the wealth of prehistoric
monuments which occur in some parts of Scotland but most
landscape features which predate the Iron Age seem to be

Aberlady Parish church. Inside is a replica of part of a Dark-Age cross
shaft found here, indicating the early origins of Christian worship on
this site.

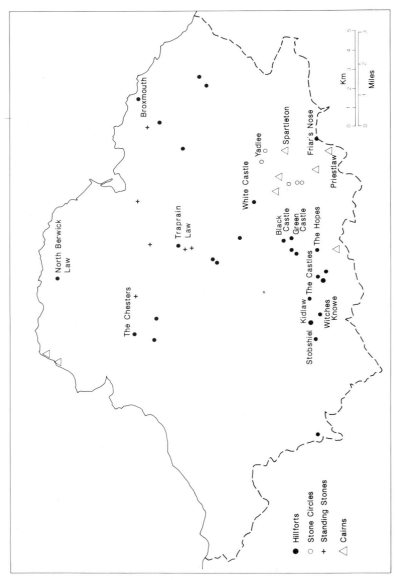

Map 4. Prehistoric Sites

linked with religion, even if the beliefs of the people who erected them remain obscure. While some of these remains are in the lowlands, it is in the Lammermuirs that the most impressive monuments have survived. These include large burial cairns, many of them on prominent hill summits, such as Spartleton Edge (653656) and Priestlaw Hill (652624), where they would have been visible from a long distance.

Even more enigmatic are the cluster of stone circles around the headwaters of the Whiteadder. Don't expect any monuments on the scale of Stonehenge, though! They are much smaller than the great stone circles and henges of the Outer Hebrides, Orkney or Southern England although they are in the same tradition. Two examples which are worth visiting lie adjacent to the B6355 between Gifford and Cranshaws. One is at Kingside Hill (627650) within a field north of the road. It is not marked on the 1:50,000 map and appears on the 1:25,000 map as an 'enclosure'. It is in fact a circle of thirty small stones about 12m in diameter. None of the stones are over ½m high; many stand on edge but some have fallen and are almost buried. Inside the circle is a low mound with a boulder on top which is probably a burial cairn. The other circle, at 629646 (not marked on either the 1:50,000 or 1:25,000 O.S. map), is smaller still but is so close to the southern side of the B6355 road that it is worth a visit. This circle has only seven surviving stones, within a low bank, surrounding a slightly hollowed interior. Other stone circles in this area are more remote and difficult of access but they are shown on Figure 4.

You might wonder why so many prehistoric monuments were built in such an apparently bleak and remote area. During the Bronze Age East Lothian's climate was rather warmer and drier than today, making these upland valleys more habitable. In addition, most of this area was forested at that time and it may have been easier for Bronze Age farmers to clear the woodlands at their uphill margins where the trees were smaller and more scattered, and the soils lighter and easier to cultivate, than to tackle the valleys with their thicker forest cover and heavier soils. On the other hand thousands of years of cultivation in the lowlands may have removed many monuments of the type which have survived in these more

B

sparsely-settled areas.

That Bronze Age man did occupy parts of the low country at least is shown by some standing stones which are so massive that nobody has taken the trouble to dig them out and topple them. While the stone circles can be linked to some kind of religious beliefs, even if we do not know their nature, these isolated standing stones are even more of a puzzle. Were they boundary stones, route markers, or meeting places? Did they commemorate people or events or did they have some astronomical significance? We shall never know for certain but this makes them all the more fascinating. Figure 4 shows the location of these stones. Three of the largest lie close to the A1. At Easter Broomhouse (680766) in a field just west of a side road off the A1 is a sandstone pillar nearly 3m high. Near its base are grooves which were made relatively recently by the wire cable attached to a steam plough, but on the west side about halfway up are much older markings: three hollows which archaeologists call 'cup marks'. These are found elsewhere on such stones although their purpose and meaning are obscure. Further west, at 616776 near Kirklandhill farm just north of the A1, is another standing stone of about the same height, clearly visible from the main road, as is the third one on the slopes of Pencraig Hill (581768), also just north of the A1, between Haddington and East Linton.

Cists, Crosses and Saints

The origins of Christianity in East Lothian lie in the Dark Age kingdom of Gododdin and, as with anything from this period, speculation is much more abundant than fact. After the Roman withdrawal Carlisle seems to have survived as a centre of Christianity and to have sent out missionaries who established a loose network of dioceses in southern Scotland. The earliest of these missionaries associated with East Lothian is the shadowy figure of St. Monenna who, according to tradition, founded a monastery on Traprain Law around A.D. 500. The hillfort capital of the Votadini (Chapter 3) was a logical place to build a church but there is, as yet, no archaeological evidence to support the existence of what would

Parish church, Pencaitland; one of East Lothian's most attractive late-medieval churches with a fine collection of old tombstones in the churchyard.

have been one of the earliest Christian churches in Scotland. Christianity certainly reached East Lothian before the Anglian invasion; this is confirmed by the discovery of many early-Christian cemeteries in the Lothians with burials laid out straight on an east-west orientation in stone-lined coffins or 'cists'. These have been discovered at various places in East Lothian. One long-cist cemetery north of Belhaven (664790) was uncovered by the sea in 1891. Apart from these early cemeteries the only tangible evidence of early Christianity is fragments of two Anglican crosses; one was formerly built into a wall of the parish church at Morham, (577726), the other (a replica of the original) is in the church at Aberlady (462799). The originals were both removed to the National Museums of Scotland in Edinburgh.

At a slightly later date, after the annexation of Lothian by the Angles of Bernicia, another missionary, St. Baldred, is recorded. Slightly more is known about him that about Monnena but much of the information is confused and contradictory. Baldred appears to have lived at two separate periods and to have been buried in at least three different places! Perhaps there were two Baldreds or a whole family of them? While one tradition makes Baldred a disciple of St. Kentigern, who established his cell at Glasgow in the late sixth century, a stronger tradition places him in the eighth century. One story is that he lived as a hermit on the Bass Rock, a lonely, rather smelly existence among the gannets. Remains of a building claimed to be his cell have been discovered on a ledge on the island but the simple rectangular chapel dedicated to him which stands near the summit dates from the sixteenth century, over 800 years after the saint died. While Baldred may well have lived on the Bass Rock for a while, he is more firmly associated with the area around Tyninghame where the fine twelfth-century church is dedicated to him. On the coast nearby a prominent rock known as St. Baldred's Cradle (638813) and St. Baldred's Boat (612849). There is a St. Baldred's Cave (605845) and the site of St. Baldred's Well near Auldhame (592845), the water of which was highly esteemed in the nineteenth century for making an excellent cup of tea!

While the vanished parish of Auldhame, and those of Tyninghame and Prestonkirk, are linked with the saint, the later chronicler Simeon of Durham claimed that Baldred ministered to the inhabitants of the area between Lammermuir (the Dunglass Burn) and the mouth of the Esk. According to one tradition Baldred died in 756 or 757 and legend has it that the inhabitants of each of his three parishes claimed the right to bury him. They were about to come to blows over it when Baldred's body miraculously multiplied into three identical corpses so that they could all be satisfied! In the following century a monastery was founded on or near the site of his cell at Tyninghame. It was a dependency of the community of St. Cuthbert at Lindisfarne. Curiously, they claimed control over lands whose limits were precisely those of the territory to whose inhabitants Baldred was supposed to have preached. This story about Baldred looks suspiciously like an attempt by the monks of Lindisfarne to strengthen their claim to the lands annexed to Tyninghame monastery!

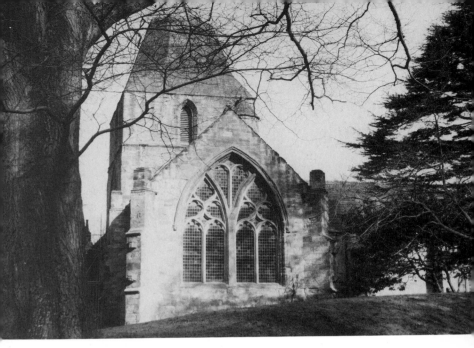

Seton collegiate church. Privately endowed by a local landowning family, this 15th and early 16th-century church survived the English invasions and the Reformation largely intact.

Old Parish Kirks

East Lothian has no cathedrals or great medieval abbeys, but although her churches are mostly modest and unassuming, they nevertheless have a wealth of interest. Exploring the county's churches often involves looking for abandoned ruins in out-of-the-way places or examining a seemingly plain, undistinguished eighteenth- or nineteenth-century building and discovering surprising and unexpected architectural features from earlier centuries. This is due to the way in which churches in this area developed over the centuries. Well-preserved early medieval churches are rare. When a church was abandoned due to a shifting of the site of the kirk, as at Gifford, or because a parish was amalgamated with another one, like Tyninghame with Whitekirk, the building has escaped later renovation or rebuilding but has usually been neglected and often robbed of its stonework, leaving a fragmentary ruin. In some cases, like the old parish church at Bara (557705), nothing remains save the site, recorded by the Ordnance

Map 5. Old Churches and Chapels

Survey, and vestiges of the old burial ground.

Where a church has been in continuous use it is usual to find that it was rebuilt as population grew and architectural tastes changed. This generally happened during the eighteenth century and often again in the Victorian era, with only vestiges of masonry from earlier periods remaining. Sometimes the rebuilding involved a new church on an adjacent site, leaving the old kirk as a ruin within the churchyard, as at Gladsmuir (458733) and North Berwick (554853), but in other cases such as Oldhamstocks (738707) and Pencaitland (444690) the new stonework was erected on the foundations of the old. This may be frustrating but it encourages some fascinating detective work.

Because of this process of evolution, remains of early medieval churches are visible in only a few parishes. The fragments of the old church at Tyninghame (619798), isolated and rather incogruous in the park around Tyninghame House, are particularly fine. The church is likely to be on or near the site of the Dark Age monastery of St. Baldred mentioned above but the structure dates from the twelfth century. The plan, with a simple rectangular nave and chancel, an apse at the eastern end and a tower at the western one, is similar to the celebrated Norman church at Dalmeny and the decoration may have been even finer. The arches of the chancel and apse still stand and have the characteristic Norman chevron pattern found at Dalmeny, while the columns of the chancel arch are richly ornamented with a fish-scale decoration. Some of the details of the stonework have parallels with churches in the East Midlands and there may be a link through King David I of Scotland. He was also Earl of Northampton and may have brought masons to Scotland from his English estates. Tyninghame church was still in good condition in the later seventeenth century but in 1761 the parish was merged with Whitekirk. The old church was largely demolished although it continued to be used as the burial place of the Earls of Haddington. The churchyard was ploughed over and the tombstones were removed, while the settlement around it was cleared and a new estate village built a kilometre away (Chapter 7).

Another early medieval church stands forlorn and abandoned in the middle of the modern resort and golfing centre of Gullane (481827). Like other twelfth-century churches in this area it has a simple rectangular nave without aisles. The chancel is narrower than the nave and a transept has been added during the fifteenth century. The chancel arch has been blocked up but you can still see the chevron design on the outside. The church was abandoned around 1612 when the Scottish Parliament authorised the transfer of the kirk to Dirleton which appears to have been prospering while Guillane was in decay, so that the church was now inconveniently located for most of the inhabitants of the parish. In addition the churchyard was being continually buried by blowing sand.

The third early East Lothian church which has been little altered is St. Martins (523739) on the eastern outskirts of Haddington. It belonged to the Cistercian nunnery of Haddington (see below) during the later twelfth century and the ruins seem to date from this time. Only the vaulted nave survives, ruined but reasonably complete. Other remains of churches from this period are mere fragments. At Garvald the church was completely remodelled in 1829 but a string-course of Norman masonry runs along the northern and western walls about 2½m above ground level. Of the old parish church at Ormiston (411676) only part of the east end survives, but built into field walls nearby are fragments of Norman chevron and dog-tooth ornament showing what happened to the stonework of this and other early churches. At Pencaitland (443690) only a shadow of the medieval church survives; the main part of the building is a simple rectangular box whose stonework is mostly sixteenth- or seventeenth-century in date. The characteristically simple early-medieval plan suggests, however, that the walls lie on much earlier foundations.

Remains of churches from later medieval times are also fragmentary though nevertheless interesting. Pencaitland parish kirk has a side chapel which may date from the thirteenth century. At Prestonkirk, on the outskirts of East Linton (592799), most of the church is a plain Georgian rebuilding of 1770 but a magnificent thirteenth-century chancel survives at the eastern end, possibly the best example of church architecture from this period anywhere in the Lothians. The ruined parish church at Keith (449645) dates

Whitekirk was a medieval pilgrimage centre and its modest, though attractive, parish kirk belies its former importance. Having survived the English wars and the Reformation, the church was burnt down by suffragettes!

mainly from this period too though the walls have been repaired and reconstructed in later times. Like Tyninghame, it stands within the grounds of the local 'big house' and was, during the twelfth century, a private chapel belonging to the Keith family. It subsequently became the parish church of Keith Marischal, but in 1618 this parish was joined to Keith Hundeby, the new parish being known as Humbie.

There are also two isolated medieval chapels at Herdmanston (472698) and on Fidra island (513869). The former was a private chapel of the Sinclairs of Herdmanston and lies within the policies of Herdmanston House. St. Nicholas' chapel on Fidra has a more obscure history. Tradition claims that there was an early Celtic monastery on this small rocky island — by no means improbable — but the earliest record relating to Fidra is around 1220 when William de Vaux, lord of Dirleton, granted the patronage of the church at Gullane to a religious house already on the island which was served by canons from Dryburgh Abbey. At a later date the de Vaux family also granted to the monks of Fidra the rest of the island and land on the mainland opposite. All that remains is a few fragments of the walls of the church and traces of foundations indicating the existence of other buildings which may have been part of the monastery.

Collegiate Churches

During the fifteenth century it became fashionable for landowners to found collegiate churches on their estates in which small groups of priests held services with more ceremony than was possible in an ordinary parish church, saying masses for the souls of the founders and their families. These private churches were often lavishly endowed and East Lothian has two of the finest examples in Scotland.

The collegiate church at Dunglass (768719) has survived substantially intact despite post-Reformation vicissitudes. Having escaped destruction during the English invasions of the 1540s, it was later converted into a barn and a stable; one gable was broken to allow access for carts, and rows of holes in the vaulting inside show where timber floors were slotted in. However, it is still an extremely attractive church, if rather severe and plain in appearance, though admittedly the windows have lost their tracery. The church is cruciform in plan with a low central tower. Inside, the nave and choir are vaulted and there is an attractive triple sedilia in the choir where the priests sat while officiating at mass. The founder, Sir Alexander Hume of Dunglass, obtained a grant of collegiate status for a church here in 1450 but there may have been an earlier private chapel on the site. The stonework suggests that the church was originally designed with only a simple nave and choir and that the tower and transepts were added later, before much of the construction work had been done.

The church at Dunglass was built more or less in one period but East Lothian's other great collegiate church at Seton (419751), is more complex. Sadly the church is not complete for the nave has vanished. It was presumably demolished after the Reformation when the church went out of use. What survive are the transepts, choir and tower of a church whose plan was similar to the one at Dunglass but whose architecture was more ornate, with a particularly fine polygonal apse end to the choir.

The neatly whitewashed church which dominates the main street of Gifford is one of the most attractive post-Reformation kirks in eastern Scotland.

There seems to have been a thirteenth-century parish church on the site, possibly represented by the foundations of the vanished nave. Around 1434 Catherine St. Clair, wife of the first Lord Seton, built a chapel whose foundations underlie the south transept. The choir was built for the third Lord Seton in the mid-fifteenth century. His successor vaulted the choir and established the church as a collegiate foundation in 1492. The fifth Lord Seton roofed the choir with stone slabs in the early sixteenth century and his widow added the transepts and tower during the 1540s. Like Dunglass, the interior is barrel-vaulted except for the crossing, above which rises a squat tower with a curious truncated spire which may never have been completed. Unlike Dunglass, which is rather dark inside, Seton is light and airy with much larger windows which have preserved their tracery. The ruins of living quarters for the priests lie between the church and Seton House.

Pilgrims and Holy Wells

Another interesting fifteenth-century church is St. Mary's at
Whitekirk. This red sandstone kirk has a solid-looking tower
with a corbelled parapet set slightly out of alignment with the
nave and vaulted chancel. There was an earlier church here for
Whitekirk was an important pilgrimage centre in medieval
times. Tales of miraculous cures from a holy well at Whitekirk
began to spread in the early fourteenth century, one of the
beneficiaries supposedly being the famous Black Agnes,
Countess of Dunbar, who defended Dunbar Castle so valiantly
against the English. By the following century large numbers of
pilgrims were visiting the well; one source claims that in 1413,
15,653 came to Whitekirk. Even if this figure is not accurate, it
suggests that it was quite a famous place, James I placed it
under his personal protection and had a set of pilgrims' hostels
built to accommodate visitors. There must have been a large
complex of buildings here alongside the church. In 1435
Whitekirk was visited by Aeneas Sylvius, a papal legate and
later Pope Plus II. He landed, possibly at Dunbar, and vowed
to walk barefoot to the nearest shrine. Unfortunately he had
not allowed for Scottish weather conditions and the chill which
he contracted in doing so left him with rheumatism for the
remainder of his life!

James IV also visited Whitekirk but in 1537 James V granted
the hostels to his favourite, Oliver Sinclair, who demolished
them and built a castle with the stones. About 100m south of
the church is a building generally considered to have been a
teind, or tithe, barn dating from the sixteenth century. The
extreme thickness of the walls at the west end of the barn
suggests that this was part of Oliver Sinclair's tower which
stood for only a few years before being burnt by the Earl of
Hertford's army in 1544 and again, for good measure, in 1548.
The remainder of the structure may be seventeenth-century in
date and probably was designed as a barn. The church survived
the destruction of English armies and the rapacity of Oliver
Sinclair but, ironically, it was burned down in 1914 by
suffragettes as a protest! Fortunately, although the interior
furnishings were lost, the fabric of the church was not seriously
damaged and the building has been skilfully restored.

What of the holy well itself? Unfortunately there is no trace left of the original well at Whitekirk. It supposedly dried up in the nineteenth century as a result of agricultural drainage operations. To find a medieval well intact you must go to Stenton. Just outside the village to the north-east you can see the remains of one of the best-preserved medieval wells in Scotland, the Rood Well (624744). It is enclosed by a small circular building with a conical roof of stone slabs which is known locally as 'The Cardinal's Hat'. Little is known about the well except that it seems to predate the Reformation. There is a tradition that the tenure of the nearby Biel estate depends on the proprietor keeping the stone roof in repair.

Burgh Kirks

While Scottish rural kirks are generally modest and homely, burgh churches are often more impressive, reflecting the greater wealth of urban communities from the fourteenth and fifteenth centuries onwards. The church of St. Mary in Haddington (519736) is one of the best examples of a late-medieval Scottish burgh kirk from a period of stability and prosperity which produced many fine buildings. It has a superb site, away from the town centre and beside the River Tyne, with ample space for a large churchyard around it. St. Mary's is not hemmed in by other buildings and this helps to emphasise its size. It is slightly bigger than St. Giles in Edinburgh and as large as many Scottish cathedrals. Unlike St. Giles, which has been altered and added to over the centuries. St. Mary's was built over a fairly short period and has not been greatly altered since.

There was a church on this site in the twelfth century but virtually all the visible stonework dates from the late fourteenth and fifteenth centuries. The church is cruciform in plan with an aisled choir and nave, and unaisled transepts. The tower may originally have been designed to carry a crown spire like St. Giles but it is unlikely that one was ever built. The medieval sacristy on the northern side was later converted into a burial place for the Maitlands of Lethington, later Dukes of Lauderdale. It contains a particularly fine monument to John Maitland, first Lord Thirlestane, his wife and his son, John,

Earl of Lauderdale. The tradition that the body of the unscrupulous Duke of Lauderdale, Secretary of State for Scotland to Charles II, does not rest in peace seems to have been caused by periodic flooding of the vault displacing his coffin! During 1548-9 when English troops fortified Haddington and a Franco-Scottish army besieged them, St. Mary's suffered a good deal of damage (Chapter 4). It lay outside the ramparts but sufficiently close to be used by Scottish and French sharpshooters. As a result the English defenders turned their cannon on it, damaging the tower and wrecking the roof and vaults. The nave was repaired after the Reformation and continued in use as a church but the transepts and choir remained in ruins until the early 1970s when they were restored with fibreglass vaults replacing the lost stone originals. The plaster vaulting in the nave was a less successful addition of 1811; originally the nave was open to the timber roof.

Dunbar also had a fine medieval kirk at the south end of the main street, built by one of the Earls of Dunbar in 1342 and elevated to collegiate status. It became the burgh kirk after the Reformation but was replaced in 1818-21 by a totally new building designed by James Gillespie Graham in a Gothic style with battlements and corner towers. Inside are monuments from the earlier church including a fine one to George Home, Earl of Dunbar, who died in 1611 having served as High Treasurer of Scotland to James VI and later Chancellor of the Exchequer after James moved south to London. Prestonpans has an attractive church dating from 1596, one of the first post-Reformation kirks to be built in Scotland, with a laird's loft for the local Hamilton family, one of whom had provided the land for the church and financed its construction. The parish church of Tranent is even later in date – 1800 – but it stands on the foundations of a substantial late fifteenth-century church with transepts and a central tower, for the medieval parish of Tranent was a large and prosperous one including the modern parishes of Prestonpans and Gladsmuir. Traces of the stonework of the old church can be seen in the south wall (including a priest's door) and the west gable while a ruined mortuary aisle for the Cadells of Cockenzie is also pre-Reformation in date.

Tranent churchyard has East Lothian's best collection of ornately-carved tombstones dating from the 17th and 18th centuries. This table-top tomb is one of the most interesting examples.

After the Reformation

Some attractive churches were built in East Lothian after the Reformation. The old parish kirk of Gladsmuir (458733) was built in 1695 with the help of money provided by the Baillies of Lamington when the new parish of Gladsmuir was created from lands taken from the parishes of Tranent, Haddington and Aberlady. It stands ruined in the churchyard next to the replacement which was built in 1838 but still has its bell cote on top of the west gable.

At Gifford the T-plan parish church, harled and whitewashed, dates from 1710 and dominates the main street of the village. The church has a square tower with a slated spire, and inside there is an attractive laird's loft complete with fireplace to allow the Tweeddales of Yester House to sit through the long sermons in comfort. The church was built to replace the old collegiate church at Bothans (544671), adjacent to Yester House, which was abandoned and left as the burial place of the Tweeddale family. The removal of the church and the settlement around it was designed to allow the policies of Yester House to be extended, and if the local people objected to this, then at least they got a fine new kirk and a neatly laid out village provided by the proprietor. In Dirleton the position of the church (512842), away from the village green beside what was probably once a cattle loan leading to the common pasture, shows that it is a comparatively recent addition to the settlement. It was built soon after 1612 to replace the medieval church at Gullane (see above).

At North Berwick as at Gladsmuir the old parish church, building of which began in 1659, and the modern replacement stand side by side (554853). But here, on the promontory by the harbour (554856), there is a third, even earlier church, dating from the twelfth century, of which only a few fragments remain. It was here that the celebrated North Berwick witches are said to have gathered in 1590, and the building was still in use as late as 1680. Much of the medieval church and its burial ground has been washed away by the sea. Originally there was a hospital here too, built to house pilgrims who were making the crossing of the Forth to the shrine at St. Andrews. Nothing is left of it though there are some fragments of the hospital which stood on the opposite shore at Earlsferry.

Churchyards

East Lothian's churchyards can be as interesting to explore as the interiors of the churches they surround. The iron jougs, designed to fit round a person's neck, which are attached to the exterior walls of churches like Garvald, Pencaitland and Spott are a reminder of the power of the kirk sessions. These were the bodies of elders who, following the Reformation, had wide powers to punish parishioners who failed to conform to the strict moral discipline which they enforced. At Pencaitland the offertory houses in the churchyard with their attractive pantiled roofs were used to shelter watchmen whose task was to prevent the activities of 'Resurrectionists' or body snatchers who dug up freshly-buried corpses to sell to the Edinburgh medical school. Spott, too, has an old watch house in the churchyard for this purpose.

Tombstones are another fascinating study. Although monuments were erected inside churches in medieval times, few outside grave markers from before the Reformation have survived. However, most East Lothian churchyards have some seventeenth-century tombstones and a wider range from the eighteenth century. There are various types; upright headstones are the most common but there are also recumbent slabs, table tombs where the slab is raised on legs, and chest tombs where the sides of a table tomb have been filled in with slabs. Their decoration varies from crude and simple to stylish and ornate but usually involves variations on a few themes symbolising death; skulls and crossbones, hourglasses or the gravedigger's shovel and pick are among the most common. Between the later seventeenth and later eighteenth centuries it was common to have the tools of a person's trade carved on his tombstone. It is interesting to go around an East Lothian churchyard trying to identify various trades from the carvings. Some are fairly obvious: the hammer and pincers of the smith, the scissors and iron of the tailor, the long-handled shovels with loaves on for a baker. Others are more obscure, such as the square and compass of the mason, and the mill rind, the piece of metal supporting the upper millstone, for a miller.

The inscriptions on the stones also record individuals and the society in which they lived. Seventeenth-century tombstones usually have short, simple inscriptions giving the name and occupation of the person, their age and the date of their death. Inscriptions are usually in the vernacular; Latin is rare, so that deciphering them is complicated only by weathering of the stone. Epitaphs on seventeenth-century tombstones are usually simple and straightforward, reflecting the faith of the people commemorated, like this one from Spott:

Death is not loss, But rather gain,
If wee by dieing, Life attain.

Others hint at the happiness and tragedies of life like the tombstone of a woman from Pencaitland;

Happie in birth, match, comely feature
And evrie vertue graceing nature
In nothing cross'd but barren womb
All that was flesh rests in this tombe.

The large numbers of babies and young children recorded on

tombstones provide grim testimony to the high level of infant mortality throughout the seventeenth and eighteenth centuries.

Eighteenth-century tombstones may carry longer inscriptions, sometimes more humorous in character like this one from Haddington:

Hout Atropos, hard hearted hag
To cut the sheugh o' Jaimie Craig
For had he lived a wheen mae years
He had been o'r teugh for all your sheirs.

Almost any East Lothian churchyard will provide a range of interesting tombstones. St. Mary's in Haddington, Pencaitland and Prestonpans have some good examples, but perhaps the best place to start with is at the parish church of Tranent (402735). There seems to have been a particularly fine school of local masons in the Tranent area and the churchyard has a good set of early stones with some especially ornate table tombs.

While the carvings and inscriptions on the tombstones of otherwise unknown people can be fascinating, it is also interesting to discover the tombstones of more famous people, sometimes in unexpected places. For instance the churchyard at Bolton contains the grave of Agnes Broun, Robert Burns' mother, and those of his sister and his brother Gilbert. After farming with Robert in Ayrshire Gilbert moved to East Lothian, working as a farm manager at Morham West Mains and later as factor to Lord Blantyre. The uncertainties of life at this time are shown by the ages of his children at their deaths; 7, 15, 18, 20 and 25.

Monks, Nuns and Friars

East Lothian did not have any great medieval abbeys but it did contain a number of priories, nunneries and friaries, some interesting traces of which remain. In Dunbar at Friarscroft (678789) a tower converted to a doocot is all that survives of a Trinitarian priory founded sometime in the mid-thirteenth century. At Luffness, outside Aberlady (471802), the foundations of a long, narrow church mark the site of a Carmelite (white) friary which was in existence by 1336. In the

Saturday shopping in Tranent.

north wall there is a recess containing a weathered effigy of a knight in thirteenth-century armour who may have been the founder. Virtually nothing survives of the other buildings of the friary but there are traces nearby of two fishponds, a common adjunct to medieval religious houses. North Berwick has the more substantial remains of a Cistercian nunnery in the grounds of an old folks' home in Old Abbey Road (548849). The nunnery was founded before 1171 but the surviving building is late-medieval and appears to be a first-floor hall, possibly the refectory and kitchen on one side of a square cloister, over a series of vaulted storage chambers. A square tower attached to the north wall is late sixteenth-century in date, having been built when the nunnery was already in ruins.

Other medieval religious houses are commemorated only by a site marked on the Ordnance Survey map or sometimes by place names. The various orders of friars, dedicated to poverty, often established themselves in or near the burghs. Haddington had a house of the Dominican (black) friars, founded in 1471, somewhere at the western end of the town, while the church of the Fransiscan (grey) friars, which is first recorded in 1242, was known as the 'Lamp of Lothian' on account of its fine stained glass. Sadly, it was burnt by the English in 1355. The friary itself was destroyed, again by the English, in 1544 and the ruins were demolished on the orders of the burgh council in 1572. On the outskirts of Haddington the Cistercian nuns had the priory of St. Mary (535747) on the north bank of the River Tyne. The road out of Haddington to the east became known as the Nungate and a suburb of the same name grew up along it on the opposite side of the river from the town. The nunnery held lands here including the church of St. Martin (see above). Adjacent to the site of the nunnery is Abbey Farm, one of whose outbuildings dates from the early sixteenth century and may have been connected with the priory in its later phases, before it was burnt in the invasion of 1544. The nearby bridge over the Tyne dates from the same period.

There were no large monasteries in East Lothian but the Cistercian abbeys of Melrose and Newbattle did own lands in the county. The Cistercians farmed their property using groups of lay brothers who lived together on farms called 'granges'. Newbattle had one such farm near Prestonpans, whose name survives as Prestongrange (375737), where they pioneered coal mining and started a long tradition of industrial activity (see Chapter 9). Melrose acquired extensive pastures in the Lammermuirs during the twelfth century. Previously these lands had been used mainly for the summer grazing of cattle but the Cistercians, who were canny businessmen as well as skilled husbandmen, turned them into huge sheep ranges based on permanent granges. The remains of one of these granges survives at Penshiel (641632) above the Fasney Water, a tributary of the Whiteadder. The name 'Penshiel' suggests that originally there were only temporary summer shieling huts here but the monks constructed a series of buildings around a courtyard as permanent accommodation for the lay brothers who shepherded their flocks on the surrounding hills. One of these, possibly fifteenth-century in date, still survives to a height of 3m or so; the ground floor has been vaulted and there are traces of an outside staircase at one corner. The courtyard lay to the south but there are also signs of other buildings, perhaps later in date, to the north.

A fascinating example of the use of a site by a religious order at two widely separated periods is Nunraw near Garvald. As the name suggests, the lands belonged to the Cistercian priory at Haddington and James II granted them the right to fortify their house there againt possible English attack. The castle of Nunraw (598707) was the result (Chapter 3). In 1547, with an English invasion imminent, the Prioress of Haddington garrisoned the castle but it was captured and held for Lord Grey of Wilton by the Laird of Brunstane (see Chapter 4). At the Reformation the lands of Nunraw came into the possession of a branch of the Hepburns but in 1946 they were bought by Cistercian monks who established on them their first new monastery in Scotland since the sixteenth century. At first they used the old castle, which had been rebuilt and extended in the nineteenth century, as their residence but from the early 1950s they began work on a completely new abbey, Sancta Maria (593700), built by the monks themselves to a plain, rather severe design which echoes early-medieval Cistercian architecture.

Reformers and Witches

East Lothian was an early centre of Protestantism and, perhaps more strangely, had one of the densest concentrations of witchcraft accusations and trials in Scotland. The most famous religious figure to come from this area was John Knox, who was born in the Giffordgate suburb of Haddington around 1512. His father was probably a burgess of Haddington though it is not known whether he was a merchant or a craftsman, and Knox was probably educated at the grammar school in the burgh. His academic success at St. Andrews University led him to be ordained as a priest at the age of 22 instead of the normal 24 but he seems to have been unable to obtain a benefice – his family were not well connected – and he was back in Haddington practising as a notary in the early 1540s. He then acted as tutor to the two sons of Sir Hugh Douglas of Longniddry and a ruined chapel near the village of Longniddry (441758) is still known as 'John Knox's church'.

While he was tutor to the Douglases he first came into contact with George Wishart, the influential preacher who openly denounced the established church and its Scottish leader, Cardinal Beaton. Wishart was able to preach openly in the Lothians because sympathetic landowners like Longniddry and the lairds of Brunstane and Ormiston, with their servants and retainers, provided a bodyguard for him. Knox formed part of this group for five weeks during which Wishart moved around preaching to large congregations at places like Inveresk and Tranent. Knox accompanied the party brandishing a huge two-handed sword. Early in January 1546 Wishart preached in St. Mary's church in Haddington to an unusually small congregation. The Earl of Bothwell, who was looking for an opportunity to seize Wishart, may have frightened people away. Wishart and his supporters spent the night at Lethington and then returned to Haddington to preach again.

By this time Wishart's supporters were beginning to melt away; they may have felt that the net was about to close in and Wishart himself seems to have had a premonition of his fate when he dismissed Knox and ordered him to return to Longniddry. Wishart went on to stay with the laird of Ormiston but was surprised there by the Earl of Bothwell with a party of soldiers. They could have defended the house against Bothwell but the earl prevented this by telling them that the cardinal was at nearby Elphinstone with a large body of men. Wishart surrendered on the promise that he should not be handed over to the cardinal; a promise which Bothwell immediately broke.

The laird of Ormiston was imprisoned but subsequently escaped. Wishart was taken to St. Andrews for examination and a few months later was burnt at the stake as a heretic. Not long after Cardinal Beaton was murdered in revenge. His killers seized and held the bishop's castle at St. Andrews for the reformed faith, being joined by many supporters including Knox and the sons of Longniddry and Ormiston. This first attempt at establishing a Reformed church in Scotland failed. Knox, after his capture at St. Andrews, was sent to the French galleys but he was able to make a triumphant return to Scotland a few years later.

High Street, Haddington.

East Lothian was also the area where the great witch-hunts of the late sixteenth and seventeenth centuries started, with the famous trials of the North Berwick witches in the 1590s. Although witchcraft had been made a crime shortly after the Reformation under a statute of 1563, prosecutions were few until 1590. It was then that the young James VI sailed to Denmark to fetch home his bride, Anne. They had a stormy return, one of their attendant vessels being sunk, but spring gales were hardly unusual. Nevertheless, rumours began to spread that the storms had been raised by witchcraft. The rumours crystallised in East Lothian after David Seaton, baillie-depute in Tranent, became suspicious about his young servant girl, Geillis Duncan, who had acquired a reputation for being able to cure sickness. Under torture she confessed to increasingly bizarre offences and named a number of accomplices including John Fian, schoolmaster at Prestonpans, and other people living as far away as Edinburgh.

When these people were examined, again under threat and torture, the stories became even more improbable. They had sailed to North Berwick in sieves. They had held gatherings of 100 or more in the churchyard there and the Devil had

John Knox: one of East
Lothian's most famous figures.

appeared to them commanding them to raise storms to destroy
the King of Scots, his greatest enemy on earth. Wax images of
King James had been moulded and other attempts made to
harm him by magic. The Earl of Bothwell, that strange,
unstable figure who posed a threat to James's life on several
occasions, was also implicated. It is hard to know what to make
of the trials; did they reflect mere rumour and panic? Were
they provoked by the King's increasing interest in witchcraft
which had probably developed from his contact with Denmark
where witch persecution was endemic? Was there a genuine
attempt to use magic against James or was it a political ploy to
frame Bothwell? We shall probably never know because details
of the trials are scanty, but they did set the pattern for the
witch persecutions which continued through the seventeenth
century. The idea of the pact with the devil and the gathering
of witches together in covens seems to have developed from the
North Berwick trials.

East Lothian was prominent in all the major witch-hunts of
the seventeenth century, notably in 1649 and 1662. Close
proximity to the judiciary in Edinburgh and the ease of
communication between ministers and kirk sessions in a

lowland area with many small parishes may help to explain this concentration of witchcraft accusations. Within the county the same places recur in records of witchcraft trials, notably Ormiston, Penston, Prestonpans, Haddington, Samuelston and Tranent. Once witchcraft had been identified in a community, through confessions, trials and burnings, it was probably easier to raise a witch-panic at a later date than in places where there was no folk-memory of witchcraft. Apart from Dunbar, cases of witchcraft in the east of the county were rarer. Many parishes do not appear at all in the annals of the Scottish witch trials and others like Tyninghame and Whittinghame produced only isolated cases. Nevertheless it was in this area, at Spott, that the last witch trial south of the Forth was initiated in 1703 with the prosecution of Marion Lille, the 'Rigwoodie (lean, tough) Witch' as she was known. The place on which she was burnt is marked by a boulder, the 'Witches Stone', besides the road to the south of the village (669752), although it has been moved slightly from the original site.

CHAPTER 3
Defence and Power

For much of its history, and indeed prehistory, the inhabitants of East Lothian felt sufficiently insecure to want to protect themselves from potential attack either by their neighbours or more distant enemies. Only within the last 350 years has society become sufficiently peaceable to encourage the inhabitants of castles and fortified houses – admittedly a minority of the population, but a powerful one – to build themselves more spacious undefended mansions.

In early prehistoric times the population of the area was so sparse, and probably so concerned with bare survival, that they did not require protection. By the Iron Age, however, a growing population was beginning to press on available resources. Society had become sufficiently developed to produce a group – chieftains or landowners – who had enough power to attack their neighbours and enough wealth to try and protect themselves behind walls and palisades. This is not to suggest that the history of the East Lothian area from the Iron Age to the seventeenth century was one of continual bloodshed, but it does indicate that there was enough periodic unrest to make it prudent for those who had the power to do so to protect themselves. The remains of their fortresses form an important element in the East Lothian landscape even today, sometimes imposing and impressive like the red curtain walls of Tantallon Castle, sometimes less obvious like the faint remains of the artillery fortifications from the English invasions of the 1540s. For the first appearance of defences in the landscape, however, we have to go back to the Iron Age.

Hillforts and Hut Circles

Forts, or hillforts, form the most impressive groups of prehistoric monuments in East Lothian. They are, nevertheless, enigmatic in many ways. A glance at their distribution in Figure 4 suggests that the term 'hillfort' is appropriate, as they are

50

The multiple ramparts of the Iron Age fort at the Chesters, near Drem, are odd in that they would have been vulnerable to attack from a nearby ridge but the high ground provides a good bird's eye view of the defences.

found mainly on isolated hills within the lowlands like Traprain Law and North Berwick Law, or crowning spurs and outliers of the Lammermuirs. This upland distribution may be misleading, though. In the 1950s the discovery from aerial photographs of a previously unknown fort at Broxmouth near Dunbar (701774) showed than even these massive and seemingly indestructible landscape features could be almost completely ploughed out by prolonged cultivation. There may well have been other such forts in the lowlands which have not yet been identified. Apart from this fort at Broxmouth and the huge one on Traprain Law there has been no systematic excavation of hillforts in East Lothian. But a good deal can be deduced from the Broxmouth excavation in particular, and enough is visible from the surface features of other forts to fit them into the general pattern which has been established from excavations elsewhere in south-east Scotland.

The Broxmouth excavation highlighted a fascinating sequence of changes which may very well have occurred at other nearby sites. It was an open, undefended settlement in the later Bronze Age. Following this the site was enclosed by two successive, roughly circular, timber palisades. Later still came a single stone wall and then several concentric earthen ramparts, the defences becoming more complex and massive through time. The final stage, which may have been contemporary with or later than the Roman occupation of southern Scotland, involved a return to an undefended settlement. This chronology has been uncovered elsewhere in south-east Scotland and it is likely that other forts in East Lothian went through a similar sequence of phases.

The switch from open to defended settlements in the early Iron Age has been linked by archaeologists to the pressure of a growing population on resources like easily-cultivated land, grazing and woodland at a time when conditions were becoming more difficult: the climate was going through a cooler and wetter phase, while soil erosion and depletion of the woodland cover, as a result of bad management of the land, was also causing problems. Under such pressures people might well have become increasingly concerned with trying to delimit and protect their property.

Palisaded enclosures like Broxmouth were clearly built when there was still plenty of timber available; it has been estimated that such a stockade would have used up the timber from two hectares of woodland. The switch to stone and earth ramparts may have reflected a growing shortage of timber as well as a need for stronger defences. The change from a single rampart to multiple ones may have been caused by the introduction of the sling. If you were defending a fort with swords and spears your best tactic was to trap your attackers in the ditch in front of the steeply-rising rampart. Sling warfare encouraged a switch to multiple defences with a massive, high inner rampart on which slingers could stand to gain maximum throwing range, with one or two lower ramparts in front to protect them. In several East Lothian forts the ramparts have this form.

The term 'fort' is rather misleading, though: it tends to make you think of purely military connotations like the American West of the French Foreign Legion. In reality most of these forts were just defended homesteads or villages. The smallest were the equivalent, in Iron Age defensive technology, of late-medieval tower houses (see below). Few East Lothian forts had a large enough area within their ramparts to be considered as real villages; in many cases the defences take up more space

Hailes Castle, deep in the valley of the River Tyne, is one of East Lothian's best-hidden fortresses but the towers and curtain walls are nevertheless formidable. In the background is Traprain Law.

than the ground they protect. Most of them did not have any internal water supplies, and this shows that for all their impressive ramparts they were only designed as protection against occasional raiding, not to withstand prolonged sieges.

The surface remains of many forts in this area suggest at least two phases of construction, and most of them have two, sometimes three, concentric ramparts enclosing a roughly circular or oval area. Figure 4 and the Ordnance Survey will help you to find many interesting forts to visit, most of them with fine views of the surrounding countryside. Two examples are particularly recommended because they are easily accessible and do not require any climbing to reach. The first is the Chesters near Drem (508783). There is limited parking by the roadside at 503783 and access to the site by a farm road. The interior is not particularly large but the defences are unusually complex and elaborate with up to five ramparts. The curious feature of this fort is that it is not sited in a good defensive position: it is closely overlooked by a ridge on which anyone could have stood and lobbed missiles into the interior. This may show that multiple ramparts were sometimes for show rather than utility. The climb up the ridge is steep and requires suitable footwear but it is worth the effort for the fine view of the fort. Inside the defences you can see the foundations of over twenty circular huts. Some of them overlie the ramparts and are clearly later than the defences.

The term 'hut' is as misleading as 'fort'. It has connotations of small size and squalor, but many of these 'huts' had diameters of up to 12m with as much floorspace as many modern two- and three-bedroomed houses. It is also hard to imagine that people who could design such complex defences could not make their homes wind and weather-proof. The second readily accessible fort is White Castle (613687) beside the minor road running south from Garvald where it climbs the steep face of the Lammermuirs. Unlike the Chesters this fort is well protected by steeply-falling ground on three sides while the easy approach from the south is blocked by three ramparts with traces of stone parapets on top.

The idea that most hillforts were only temporary refuges has been abandoned in favour of the theory that they were more permanently settled, but some forts on the edge of the Lammermuirs are so exposed and high-lying that it is difficult to imagine them being comfortable in winter, especially as Iron Age weather conditions are likely to have been no better, and possibly worse, than today's. Another possibility is that they were inhabited mainly in summer when cattle were driven up from the lowlands to the hill grazings. Cattle may have been corralled between the ramparts because finds of bones from Broxmouth, coupled with the apparent lack of cultivation around the forts in the Lammermuirs, suggest that the inhabitants were more concerned with cattle ranching than with raising crops.

It is not certain when the forts went out of use. The coming of the Romans is a popular watershed, but the defences at Broxmouth had been abandoned well before this date. At some forts, like the Chesters and Black Castle (712718), there are foundations of cicular stone houses overlying the ramparts which probably relate to occupation during Roman or post-Roman times.

Dirleton Castle, the epitome of a medieval fortress, stands on one side of an attractive green around which the village of Dirleton is laid out.

Traprain Law: A Tribal Capital

One fort in a special category is the one on Traprain Law (582748). Most East Lothian forts only enclosed an area large enough for a few families. The ramparts of Traprain, at their maximum extent, defended an area of 17ha (42 acres), making it, along with the fort on Eildon Hill North, the largest in south-east Scotland – a veritable town. Traprain must have been a major centre of wealth and power; archaeologists believe it was the capital of a tribe known to the Romans as the Votadini who occupied much of the Lothians and Berwickshire. The site was well chosen, for Traprain is visible over much of East Lothian, a perpetual symbol of authority to the communities in the forts along the edge of the Lammermuirs who could look across the intervening country at it.

Although you can trace the remains of the ramparts on many parts of the hill, the fort is so large that it is hard to get a good impression of it – though the view from the summit is well worth the climb. Parts of the fort were excavated early this century and a large quantity of pottery and metalwork was

discovered. Although the dig was rather haphazard, it revealed
the bare outlines of the settlement's development. It began
modestly in late Bronze Age times with a rampart enclosing
only 4ha (10 acres). A more substantial stone rampart was built
about 700 B.C. taking in an area twice as large. About the first
century A.D. the lower western slopes of the hill were brought
within the defences. The fort reached its maximum extent
about A.D. 300 and was later contracted to enclose an area of
about 12ha (30 acres). At its peak Traprain must have had a
substantial population, for excavations revealed one area in
which a group of rectangular houses was arranged on either
side of a narrow street and around a small square.

The fact that the fort on Traprain Law remained occupied
during the Roman annexation of southern Scotland suggests
that relations between the Votadini and the Romans were
good. If you look at a map of Roman forts and roads in
Scotland, the south-eastern corner – the territory of the
Votadini – is a conspicuous blank. There are no known Roman
sites east of Dere Street, running from the Roman fort at
Newstead near Melrose to their base at Inveresk. This has
been interpreted as indicating that the Votadini did not need
policing by the Romans and may have negotiated a treaty
which allowed them to keep their capital intact. Inveresk
(342719) is the only Roman site within East Lothian. The fort,
which stands on a terrace above a bend in the River Esk only a
kilometre from the sea, partly underlies the later parish church
and churchyard, but there is virtually nothing to see of it on
the surface.

Peaceful relations with the Romans are also suggested by
finds of Roman pottery at Traprain and elsewhere in East
Lothian. Traprain appears to have been abandoned for a
generation or more during the late second and early third
centuries A.D., coinciding with the withdrawal of the Romans
from their frontier on the Antonine wall between the Forth
and Clyde estuaries. The Votadini may have suffered at this
period, like the Romans, from incursions by tribes from north
of the Forth. Despite this the Votadini seem to have retained
their close links with the Romans when they re-established
control over southern Scotland. The most fascinating discovery
from Traprain was the finding in 1919 of a large hoard of
silver beneath one of the huts. The silver included plates, bowls

The red curtain walls of Tantallon Castle, set on a clifftop and looking towards the Bass Rock, have the most dramatic setting of any of East Lothian's medieval fortresses.

and other vessels all of which had been flattened and cut up as if ready for smelting and recasting. The silver was Roman in origin and it was originally thought that it had been looted from a Roman settlement further south. It is more likely, however, bearing in mind the close links between the Votadini and the Romans, that this was some kind of payment to a native chief, either for providing troops to help guard the frontier or to keep him loyal.

Doon Hill: An Anglian Palace

For about 300 years during the Dark Ages the area which became East Lothian was dominated by the Anglian kingdom of Bernicia (later Northumbria). Although the Angles held this area for such a long period, traces of their occupation are elusive (see Chapter 7). However, on Doon Hill (686755), whose steep northern face overlooks the village of Spott, aerial photographs revealed an Anglian-period site which was excavated in the 1960s.

The remains were of two superimposed timber halls, each enclosed by a polygonal wooden palisade. The later hall paralleled almost exactly the seventh-century hall of King Oswy of Northumbria at Yeavering in Northumberland and must have been close to it in date. The earlier hall at Doon Hill, dating from the sixth century, was similar to the later one in its proportions but very different in its carpentry techniques, with unusual V-shaped protruding gable ends which have not so far

C

been matched elsewhere. This first hall, which had been occupied for at least fifty years and perhaps for as much as a century, seemed to reflect Anglian influence in its design while preserving its own distinctive local style and techniques. It is thought that it was built for a British tribal ruler. This hall was burnt down and the second, Anglian, hall was built to replace it immediately after. Here we have clear evidence of a violent initial conquest followed by a takeover which emphasised continuity in the site and style of building and probably in the management of the surrounding lands. The foundations of the halls and their enclosing walls have been marked out on the ground, and from the summit of the hill, a short distance away, there is a fine view of the site of the battle of Dunbar in 1650 (Chapter 4).

Medieval Castles

The settlement of many Anglo-Norman families in Scotland in the twelfth and thirteenth centuries under the patronage of kings like David I brought with it a new system of landholding – feudalism – and new techniques of defence. The colonists introduced the earth and timber motte-and-bailey castle which had become the standard form of defence in England. Although some Norman families received grants of land in East Lothian at an early date, no mottes have survived. It is possible that few were built here, for they are more characteristic of frontier areas like Galloway and the North-East where the new feudal lords required a secure base from which to control their estates. The subterranean "Goblin Ha" at Yester (see below) may have been dug into the earthen motte of an earlier timber castle. There are also hints of long-vanished mottes in historical documents – one at Gladsmuir was still visible in the seventeenth century, while the 'old castle' at Eldbotle which preceded the stone castle of Dirleton may also have been of earth and timber construction. Elsewhere timber or stone halls with lighter defences may have been the normal dwelling for many landowners.

By the later twelfth century castle design in Scotland was becoming more sophisticated as techniques of siege warfare

The simple fortified house of Johnscleuch, deep in the Lammermuirs, is a reminder of how the houses of many small lairds would have looked 400 years ago.

grew more effective. East Lothian has no examples of early stone castles where a simple curtain wall ringed an enclosure containing the lord's hall and other buildings, sometimes with a central stone keep. However, there are some fine examples of the more developed 'castles of enclosure' where a massive curtain wall was further strengthened by strong towers and gatehouses which provided much of the accommodation for the castellan and his retainers.

Some of these castles, besides being the homes of great magnates and the centres from which their estates were run, were also of great strategic importance for Scotland as a whole. The most strategically significant medieval castle in East Lothian, at Dunbar (678794) is, sadly, the least impressive today. Dunbar was the gateway to the Lothians for all armies invading by the east-coast route. Holding the castle was vital to the defence of eastern Scotland, losing it to the English was a major disaster. This explains the ambivalent attitude which Scottish monarchs sometimes had to Dunbar Castle: should it be garrisoned against possible invasion or destroyed to prevent the enemy gaining a valuable holding point? The castle was

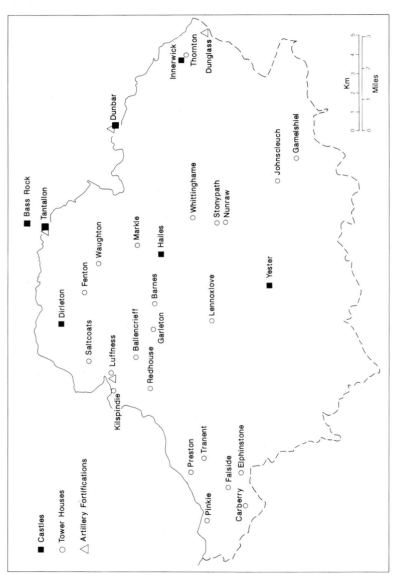

Map 6. Castles, Towers and Fortifications.

demolished in 1488 after being annexed to the Crown, but only a dozen years later James IV decided to have it rebuilt when war threatened. Despite this rebuilding and further improvements in the early sixteenth century the castle was in a dilapidated state fifty years later when French forces strengthened it with earthworks. These were dismantled in 1560 in accordance with the Treaty of Leith and the castle itself was ordered to be demolished by the Regent Moray in 1567 after the abdication of Mary Queen of Scots because her husband, the Earl of Bothwell, had used it as a base.

All that remain of the castle are a few stumps of walling on the crags at the entrance to the new harbour. These give a poor impression of its former size or the strength of its position. The building of the harbour destroyed part of the castle. Most of the visible stonework dates from the fifteenth and sixteenth centuries rather than earlier periods. It was a castle of enclosure with a strong curtain wall and a gatehouse or barbican of which only a few fragments remain. On an adjacent promontory to the south-west are the remains of an early artillery battery which was linked to the castle by a massive masonry bridge containing an internal passageway which spanned the intervening inlet. This, however, dates from the sixteenth century. You must exercise your imagination to visualise the earlier castle which was so stoutly defended against the Earl of Salisbury in 1339 by 'Black Agnes', Countess of March, the redoubtable daughter of Randolph, Earl of Moray, one of Robert Bruce's commanders. The garrison held out for nineteen weeks despite the siege engines which the English troops brought against it. Tradition has it that when catapulted stones hit the castle, Agnes coolly ordered her maids to go round the walls with their handkerchiefs to remove the dust, the only damage that the missiles had caused!

The most secluded of East Lothian's medieval castles is Hailes (575758). Its situation is surprising, hidden deep in the valley of the River Tyne in its gorge section above East Linton, but its site is strong enough, overlooking a steep drop to the Tyne on the north, and protected by the ravine of a tributary to the west and south. The earliest fortification on this site may have been a small stone manor house built in the thirteenth century. Houses of this type were probably quite common in

Scotland before the advent of the tower house (see below), but few have survived. The Hepburns of Hailes extended it in the following century into a full curtain-wall castle with a roughly rectangular layout.

The remains which are visible today consist mainly of the northern part of the curtain wall linking two rectangular towers which, although ruined, still stand over 12m high. One tower overlooks the junction of the ravine with the river at the western end of the castle. The other rises above the river bank further to the east. The curtain wall continued eastwards beyond this second tower with a staircase leading down to a landing above the river and a postern gate in the north-eastern corner. From the western tower the curtain wall curves around with the main entrance in the south wall but the rest of the circuit is broken. The castle was partly demolished by Cromwell in 1650. There are indications of another tower, a circular one, halfway along the southern side of the castle. Within the curtain wall a three-storey range of buildings links the two towers, but is probably of a later date. Hailes was the seat of the Hepburn family who later achieved prominence and notoriety as the Earls of Bothwell.

More intact than Hailes or Dunbar is Dirleton Castle (515839). It is difficult to appreciate its massive strength at first because it stands in such a peaceful setting, surrounded by well-tended lawns with the village green and neat cottages of Dirleton just beyond. The site here is a craggy outcrop in otherwise flat country, an outcrop whose steepness has been increased by quarrying and digging. Although the curtain wall on the western side has been removed almost to its foundations, the rest of the castle is well preserved. Its massive round towers, deep rock-cut ditch, and drawbridge are closer to the image of a medieval castle which most of us acquire as children than any other fortress in this area.

The original castle was erected by the de Vaux family, Anglo-Norman incomers who moved to Scotland with the encouragment of David I in the mid-twelfth century and who acquired lands in this area in the early thirteenth century. Their first castle may have been an earth and timber one here or at Eldbotle a short distance away. During the thirteenth century this was replaced by a stone castle consisting of three

Redhouse Tower, south of Aberlady, has preserved its encircling defensive wall, or barmkin, along with a range of outbuildings and a doocot.

huge round towers and two smaller ones linked by a curtain wall. In 1298, during the Wars of Independence, the castle was besieged by the Bishop of Durham with a section of Edward I's army. The garrison held out for a long time until the besiegers had been reinforced with more effective seige engines. After its capture the English garrisoned it until 1311, but when the Scots eventually regained the castle substantial parts of it were demolished by order of Robert Bruce to deny the enemy a potential holding point. In the later fourteenth century it came into the hands of the Halyburtons who carried out a major rebuilding programme which produced the castle more or less as it appears today.

You approach the castle from the west, and even here the ruin of the curtain wall is impressive with a long winding flight of steps leading up to a gap in the walls. Once you turn the corner towards the south the full power of the castle is apparent. The ditch is cut deep in solid rock and beyond it rises the great thirteenth-century drum tower dating from the first phase of construction. This tower was effectively the keep with a hall for the lord of the castle on one level and accommodation for the garrison below. Beyond this a wooden footbridge angles up towards the high fourteenth-century entrance with its lofty arch. Originally the ditch was spanned by a drawbridge. Most of the castle from the entrance round to the north side dates from the rebuilding by the Halyburtons during the fourteenth and fifteenth centuries, but you can see the remains of the bases of two more great towers from the thirteenth-century de Vaux castle. This wing housed the main hall at first-floor level with the kitchens at one end and private chambers at the other. Below the hall were storage areas and underneath the private apartments a chapel with, rather inappropriately, a prison beneath it.

The castle last saw action during Cromwell's invasion of 1650. After the battle of Dunbar (Chapter 4) Cromwell controlled most of the county but small bands of royalist cavalry held out at Dirleton and Tantallon. Cromwell sent Major-General Lambert against Dirleton with 1,600 men and a train of artillery. Dirleton may have been difficult to assault with medieval siege engines, but the improved cannon of the seventeenth century were a different matter. The first few shots bought down the gate and drawbridge, killing one of the leaders of the garrison; the rest promptly surrendered, leaving Lambert to demolish the castle.

Most impressive of all East Lothian's castles, for its magnificent clifftop site looking towards the Bass Rock as well as for its air of impregnability, is Tantallon (596851). An old local saying, 'ding doon Tantallon, mak a brig to the Bass', expressed two seemingly impossible feats and, indeed, before the period when its fortifications became obsolete, nobody did succeed in 'dinging doon' Tantallon. Even Cromwell's forces under General Monk had a difficult task capturing it in 1650, by which time it was in a decrepit state and was defended by less than a hundred men. They only surrendered after a twelve-day bombardment.

If you were to imagine an ideal coastal location for a medieval castle, this is the kind of position you would pick; a narrow peninsula, easily defended, and sheer cliffs on all other sides with the crash of waves on the rocks below mingling with the cries of the seabirds. The site is similar to that of Dunbar Castle but there has been less destruction and deterioration.

Whittinghame Tower, among the foothills of the Lammermuirs, is a good example of the basic type of tower house which elsewhere in East Lothian has been obscured by later additions and extensions.

Although parts of Tantallon have gone over the cliff, the landward curtain wall is still a daunting sight. In layout, Tantallon is a castle of enclosure with all the defences concentrated on the landward side. The sheer drop to the sea on the other three sides made substantial defences unnessary. You approach it through a series of outworks, the most striking of which is a great ditch with ramparts on either side and a gateway defended by a wall and round tower. Beyond this is the bailey, and between this and the castle there is a further rock-cut ditch. Above the ditch rises the castle itself, mostly dating from the fourteenth century, roughly contemporary with the main rebuilding at Dirleton. The landward facade consists of a central tower and two flanking ones linked by a high curtain wall. The central tower was altered during the sixteenth century with a new forework.

Tantallon was the chief stronghold of the powerful Douglas family, and its impregnability helped them on more than one occasion to defy the Crown with impunity. Archibald Douglas, fifth earl of Angus, who had engaged in treasonable correspondence with the King of England, refused to surrender to James IV who beseiged him here in 1491 with an artillery train brought from Edinburgh and Linlithgow. The king's forces achieved little and a reconciliation with Angus was eventually arranged. In 1528 history repeated itself; the sixth earl of Angus, who had married Margaret, daughter of Henry VIII and widow of James IV, fell under suspicion of being in league with Henry against James V. James laid siege to Tantallon, but after twenty days of bombardment his artillery had made little impression on the walls and he gave up. Angus then cheekily sallied out and captured the artillery as it was being slowly trundled away!

Two other medieval curtain-wall castles in East Lothian, although badly ruined, are nevertheless interesting. Innerwick Castle (735737) stands of the edge of a deep ravine cut by the Thornton Burn which surrounds it on three sides. The neck of the promontory has been cut off by a deep ditch. The buildings are in a poor state due to Protector Somerset. When he advanced into Scotland in 1547 the castle, which belonged to a branch of the Hamiltons, was held by the Master of Hamilton and a handful of men who made a brave attempt at defending it. They were overwhelmed by superior numbers and the castle, which commanded the main route into England along which Somerset's reinforcements and supplies had to be brought, was demolished to remove the threat. There are no indications that the visible remains are any earlier than the fifteenth century, but the walls which enclose the promontory probably replaced earlier ones.

The most mysterious of all East Lothian's early castles is Yester (557667). Its site is like that of Innerwick; a promontory above the stream with the ground falling steeply on three sides and the promontory cut off by a massive ditch. The site is even narrower than at Innerwick and only a few fragments of the curtain wall remain. The most fascinating remnant of the castle is a large underground hall some 6m long with a pointed barrel vault. This is the famous "Goblin Ha'", constructed by Sir Hugo de Gifford, supposedly a wizard, with the aid of a supernatural familiar or goblin. Gifford died in 1267 and the underground vault can be interpreted as the undercroft or lowest storey of a keep.

Saltcoats Castle, near Dirleton, is notable for its elaborately corbelled towers and for the high quality of its decoration.

Tower Houses

The great baronial castles of East Lothian are few in number; the average laird did not live in anything as grand as Dirleton or Tantallon. Between the fourteenth and seventeenth centuries the normal residence for all but the greatest proprietors was a tower house. The idea of the tower seems to have developed in the fourteenth century when curtain-wall castles were going out of fashion as being too expensive to build in a country crippled by war and internal dissension. The Goblin Ha' at Yester Castle may be the remains of one of the earliest known examples, but most of East Lothian's towers date from the fifteenth and sixteenth centuries.

At the core of a medieval castle like Dirleton was a large hall, usually with the private chambers of the lord at one end, the kitchens at the other and storage space in an undercroft below. The tower house took these elements – storage, hall and private quarters – and arranged them vertically one above the other, enclosing them within a defensive shell so that the minimum possible ground area was exposed to attack. The idea was simple but effective and the plan was flexible enough to serve landowners large and small. Tower houses were also durable, and while most were only designed to withstand small-scale raiding, they often proved formidable obstacles to larger armies. At one time almost every landowner with any pretensions lived in one and many are still visible in varying degrees of alteration and preservation. Some are still inhabited; others stand ruined, either alone in open country or adjacent to later farmsteads which have been built from their tumbled stonework, their former courtyards filled with old rusting agricultural machinery. Some, like the badly ruined tower which stands close to the centre of Tranent (405730), have been engulfed by later buildings. Many have vanished altogether, only their sites being marked on the Ordnance Survey map. Figure 5 shows those towers which are in a reasonable state of preservation and are worth a detour to see, as well as those which are badly ruined but which you may like to visit if you are in the vicinity.

Although they differed in detail, East Lothian's tower houses were built to a fairly standard pattern and, as with the county's old churches, much of the fascination of visiting them lies in discovering the minor variations which make each one distinctive. The normal internal layout of a tower house was three storeys, the lowest sealed by a single or double stone vault, with possibly further vaults above. The basement was used for storage and often had no direct communication with the floors above save for a small hatch in the vault. From near the entrance a circular staircase ran to the first-floor hall but the floor above, with the private accommodation, was often reached by a separate staircase projecting out in a turret. This was a further hindrance to would-be attackers who had forced the stout wooden door and iron grille or 'yett' at the base of the tower. Above the private rooms the staircase led to a parapet walk, and there was usually further accommodation in an attic storey on the inside of the wall-walk. Towers were largely passive in their defences; the few apertures in the walls were mainly for ventilation. The only way attackers could be threatened was from the battlemented parapet which usually

Preston Tower, near Prestonpans. The additional accommodation above the original parapet walk was added when the owners ran out of space!

projected outwards on corbels with gaps or machicolations which allowed the defenders to drop missiles on anyone assaulting the base of the walls.

The domestic nature of many towers is shown by their central location within their estates on sites which were not obviously defensive. Some, like Fenton Tower near North Berwick (544821) or Elphinstone Tower outside Tranent (390699), have commanding sites on exposed ridge-tops, while others such as Markle (579775) take advantage of small rocky outcrops. Relatively few, however, have sites which are difficult of access or have been artificially strengthened. In this category comes Stoneypath Tower (597714), on a promontory above the Papana Water with steep slopes on three sides and an earth rampart on the fourth. Stoneypath, an early tower dating from the fifteenth century, has its original entrance at first-floor level, reached by an external staircase, making it even harder to attack.

It is a mistake, however, to consider East Lothian's towers as purely military works; first and foremost they were landowner's homes, the centres from which their estates were run. The hall which usually occupied the first floor of a tower might be used to hold the baron court, the local instrument of justice, over which the proprietor presided. In some towers like Lennoxlove and Falside the lowest chamber in a wing of the tower or elswhere in the basement was probably used as a prison; the one at Lennoxlove is barely lit by a small flue and only connects with the room above by a hatch in the vault. This may sound despotic and cruel, but as the lowest level of law enforcement, landowners whose estates were erected into baronies had the right, until well into the eighteenth century, of pit and gallows: to imprison and execute. By the later sixteenth century the latter power was rarely exercised but the former was still used.

Because East Lothian was so prosperous, most early towers have been enlarged, replaced or incorporated within the fabric of later houses. Many later mansions like Biel (637759) and Luffness (476804) have early tower houses at their cores. As a result there are few of the small, starkly simple towers that are common in the Border dales. A good example of a fortified house at is most basic is Johnscleuch (631664) in the heart of the Lammermuirs, clearly visible from the road between Garvald and Cranshaws. Here the tower, still occupied as a farmhouse, is a simple, rectangular, two-storey building with a staircase in a semi-circular tower protruding from one of the side walls. There are no windows in the ground floor which originally consisted of two vaulted chambers with a huge chimney in the east gable for the kitchen fireplace. Although the house may originally have had a third storey, it is still a good example of the simpler type of tower belonging to a landowning family of modest means, in this case a branch of the Lauders. It probably dates from the early seventeenth century, a period when fortification was going out of fashion in the lowland part of the county but when protection was still evidently needed in this more remote upland district.

Some older fifteenth-century towers were taller, thicker-walled and much more imposing than Johnscleuch. Elphinstone Tower, near Tranent (391699), was a good example with massive walls honeycombed with small rooms and chambers leading off the main apartments. Although there were only three main storeys, the height of the vaults suggests there were extra timber floors between giving six levels up to

Hospitality, country style, at the Longniddry Inn.

the parapet walk nearly 18m above ground level. Elphinstone, well protected against raid or siege, was unable to withstand the effects of mining subsidence and much of the castle was demolished for safety after the walls had cracked badly. Another early tower, one which is open to the public, forms the core of Lennoxlove House near Haddington (515720). The tower has three main floors below the parapet walk whose machicolations have been blocked up at a later date and replaced by loopholes for muskets. The windows in the tower are larger than they would have been in the fifteenth century and a panel records that John Maitland, Earl of Lauder, enlarged them and widened the staircase in 1626, by which date the need for defence was dying out.

A number of early towers like Elphinstone and Falside (378710) had square or rectangular plans but many had their layouts altered by extensions while later towers adopted more sophisticated layouts from scratch. This increased the space available within them and improved their defensive capabilities. A common development was an L-plan, as at Lennoxlove and Stoneypath. In such arrangements the staircase could be placed

71

in the wing and the main block, allowing it to be defended more effectively from the parapet or from gun loops in the lower halls. An even more refined layout was the Z-plan, which can be seen at Nunraw (589707), where two square towers project from opposite angles of the rectangular main block.

Tower houses did not stand in isolation. They were generally surrounded by a stone wall or barmkin enclosing a courtyard with the tower on one side and ranges of outbuildings on the others. If, in a sense, the tower is a poor man's version of the keep of a medieval castle, then the barmkin is a scaled-down imitation of the curtain wall. The barmkin might be provided with gunloops and could be defended at need but its prime function was to provide refuge for livestock in time of danger; both the courtyard and the outbuildings were expendable, and if a large attacking force appeared, the defenders would abandon them and retreat into the tower.

While many towers survive, most barmkins have been removed in later landscaping alterations. At Lennoxlove only the fine Renaissance gateway remains. The courtyard and outbuildings can still be traced around some ruined towers, though. The most interesting in layout is probably Barnes Castle (529766) at the eastern end of the Garleton Hills, known locally as The Vaults and built for John Seton of Barnes in the 1590s. The plan is imposing and advanced for its period, the house being rectangular with large square towers projecting from the corners. The barmkin also had towers at the corners and midway along the walls, but it is not clear to what extent they were designed to be ornamental or defensive. The main block never seems to have been completed above the level of the ground-floor vaults. At Garleton Castle (509768), only a couple of kilometres away, you can see the vestiges of a less regular barmkin and outbuildings. Only fragments of the tower remain but at the south-west side of the ruined courtyard there is a two-storey lodge with a projecting turret staircase on the outer side and a later outside forestair within the courtyard. At the north-west angle of a more modern building stands on the foundations of a second outbuilding. The best-preserved barmkin and outbuildings are at Redhouse, south of Aberlady (463770). Here the fine sixteenth-century gateway has a row of projecting corbels above the arch suggesting that there may once have been a gatehouse on top. The range of outbuildings on the east side of the courtyard is largely intact with a dovecote incorporated in the upper storey.

By the later sixteenth century the grim, functional lines of many East Lothian towers were being softened and embellished by increased decoration. Because of a continuing need for defence much of this was confined to the upper parts of the walls. Saltcoats Castle near Gullane (485819), dating from the late sixteenth century, is a good example. Much of the castle is in ruins but the western end of the main block has some interesting features. Two towers protruding from the corners are round at ground level but are corbelled out into a larger square section above and are joined near the top with a stone arch. This arch echoes the ones at Hermitage Castle in Liddesdale which were designed to carry a machicolated parapet across the gap between the towers. At Saltcoats the arch is purely decorative, though, as is the row of closely-set gargoyles above it. Even the gun loops are ornamental rather than functional.

Towers were often cramped inside and various expedients were adopted to increase the amount of space. Sometimes a massive extension was made, as at Falside (378710) where the rectangular fifteenth-century tower was doubled in size by an L-shaped addition in the following century. At Preston Tower (379739) the novel idea of adding two storeys of apartments above the original parapet walk was tried in a seventeenth-century alteration. The effect was to produce an imposing double-decker tower with a top-heavy appearance.

Artillery Fortifications

During the late fifteenth and sixteenth centuries the development of artillery began to change Scottish fortifications in two main ways. Castles had to be altered to accommodate cannon for use by the defenders, and new methods of defence had to be adopted to counteract bombardment by attackers. One of the earliest purpose-built artillery fortifications in Scotland is at Dunbar. A short way south-west of the main castle is a second rocky peninsula on which has been built a polygonal block-house designed for cannon on two levels – firing from a parapet above and casements below. This blockhouse was built between 1515 and 1523 for the Duke of Albany, regent of Scotland after James IV was killed at Flodden. The strategic importance of Dunbar had grown since the loss of Berwick in 1482, and Albany made Dunbar his main base. The new blockhouse was connected to the castle in a novel way: by a wall containing an internal passageway, which arched out across the intervening inlet of the sea. Parts of it can still be seen.

Elsewhere the impact of artillery was limited. At Tantallon the east tower was pierced with wide-mouthed gun loops, as were the wall and gate tower beyond the bailey. These new defences seem to have been in place by the time of the royal siege of 1528, and the rampart defending the bailey may have been heightened to act as a shock absorber to soak up cannon fire and protect the base of the curtain wall behind. If so, then it was very effective. Beyond the bailey is a further artillery fortification, an arrowhead-shaped earthwork known as a 'ravelin', an outer defence with an open back so that if it had to be abandoned it was exposed to fire from the castle and could not be held against the defenders. The date of this earthwork is unknown but it is certainly later than the early sixteenth century.

The campaigns in East Lothian during 1547-49 gave rise to a new set of forts built by the Scots and their French allies on the one hand and the English on the other. Existing castles like Hailes and Ormiston were pressed into service as local garrisons which could resist raids by small groups of horsemen and infantry, but new bastioned forts were also built. The largest of these were the defences thrown up around Haddington by the English garrison which dug in there and held out against the French and Scottish forces in 1548 and 1549 (see Chapter 4). The defences were built in a hurry, largely of earth and timber rather than stone, which perhaps explains why they have not survived. Traces of them were still visible in the early eighteenth century, for Daniel Defoe wrote that the remains of four large bastions could be seen.

When the French forces besieged the English garrison in Haddington they brought their artillery by sea from Leith to Aberlady and constructed a fort there in 1549 to prevent the English fleet from landing supplies and men for the relief of the town. The remains of this fort can still be seen around

Gullane has not one but three golf courses. This is the scene at the first tee on No. 1.

Luffness House (476805) as a wide ditch and various mounds. The fort was dismantled on the orders of Mary of Guise in 1552. More impressive and accessible is another English fort in the east of the county. The Ordnance Survey mark a site at 763718 on a steep-sided promontory overlooking the deeply-cut valley of the Dunglass Burn as 'French Camp' but it was in fact constructed by English forces under the command of Lord Grey of Wilton. The fort is a fairly small one and recent research on plans in the Duke of Rutland's collection suggests that it was only part of a more extensive system of fortifications around Dunglass. The area around the church was trenched to form a fortified camp defended on the east by the fort which can be seen today. There may also have been a larger and more sophisticated fort on the coast at 771726 just to the north of the mouth of the Dunglass Burn. This fort, clearly illustrated on a contemporary plan, has had its earthen ramparts completely levelled by four centuries of cultivation. It served as a staging post on the dangerous route between Berwick and the garrison at Haddington. It was too close to the Border for French or Scottish forces to attack and it provided a forward base from which convoys of provisions, arms and ammunition could be hurried to Haddington. After the Treaty of Boulogne in 1550 ended hostilities it was evacuated by its garrison and handed back to the Scots who dismantled it.

Later fortifications are rare in East Lothian although there is an eighteenth-century gun battery at the entrance to the old harbour of Dunbar (Chapter 10). During the Second World War it was thought that East Lothian's low, sandy coasts might make good landing places for the enemy. Thousands of huge, closely-spaced concrete blocks were built around the shores of bays like Gosford and Belhaven to prevent tanks and other vehicles from getting ashore. Pillboxes also were built every so often. Most of the concrete blocks have been removed, greatly improving the appearance of many beaches, but you can still find some of them in more remote locations like the shore north of Belhaven.

CHAPTER 4
Battle, War and Siege

East Lothian did not always benefit from contact with England. For many centuries it was dangerously close to the Border, on the easiest invasion route, one which, in contrast to the west coast, led through well-settled lowlands nearly all the way, straight to the capital and the heart of Scotland. Along this route an invading army could march comfortably, supplied by sea as it went. The one difficult section was the valley of the Pease Burn (7970) and the gorge of the Dunglass Burn (7671) on the boundary of East Lothian. Daniel Defoe, a sharp observer, thought that 1,000 well-led men positioned there could hold back an army. This rarely happened, though: the route from Berwick was too short for forces from the Lothians to respond in time and hold this strategic pass. The area near Dunbar where the East Lothian plain first opens out, or closer to Edinburgh near the crossing of the Esk, were the places along the invasion route where battles were usually fought.

The East Lothian countryside often bore the brunt of devastation. The outlines of medieval campaigns, such as the Wars of Independence, are sketchy and the landscape has changed so much since then that it is difficult to appreciate how it directed the strategy and tactics of the military commanders. From the sixteenth century onwards, however, records are more detailed, allowing us to reconstruct what happened more accurately and enabling us to relate past events to the present-day landscape. This chapter looks at some notable battles and sieges in East Lothian from the sixteenth, seventeenth and eighteenth centuries and relates them to the modern landscape.

The Battle of Pinkie, 10th September 1547 (361717)

In 1544 and 1545 Henry VIII sent the Earl of Hertford to invade Scotland to try and force the Scots to agree to the marriage of the infant Mary with his son Edward, a process

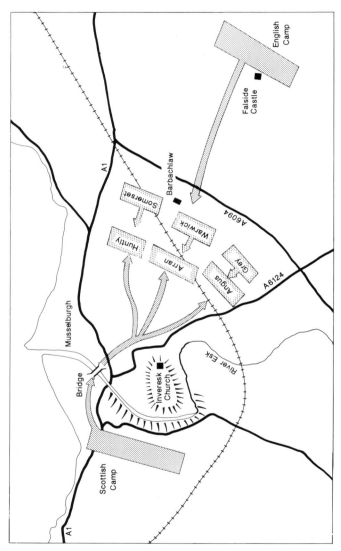

Map 7. The Battle of Pinkie, 1547.

which became known as the 'Rough Wooing'. By the summer of 1547 Henry was dead and Hertford, now Duke of Somerset, was regent to the young Edward VI. He still favoured the marriage, and when negotiations broke down he invaded Scotland with an army of about 16,000 men supported by a fleet. The Scots had collected a larger army: perhaps 25,000 men, but less experienced, less well equipped and less professionally led. Somerset drew up his forces on the ridge of Falside Hill overlooking the Esk valley with his centre near Falside Castle (378710) and his right flank close to the sea protected by his fleet. This extended line was perhaps designed to give the Scots a false impression of the size of the English army. The Scots faced him to the west of the Esk in a strong defensive position with the river in front of them, a marsh on their right and the sea to their left. On the seaward side they had thrown up a turf wall to protect themselves from the guns of the English fleet. The Regent Arran commanded the army with the Earl of Angus in charge of the centre and Lord Huntly on the right.

On the morning of 10th September, 'Black Saturday' as the Scots were to christen it, having assessed the strength of the Scottish position, Somerset began to move his men to lower ground to get his artillery into range and to probe for a way to attack the Scots. He took up a line roughly parallel with and a little north-west of the A6094 road between Wallyford and Whitecraig, with his left wing near Sweethope (355708) and his right near Barbachlaw (363719). Somerset's intention may have been to occupy the low hill by the river on which Inveresk church stood. From there he could command much of the Scottish line before launching his attack. The English were then astonished to see the Scots leave their defensive position, crossing the Esk by the stone bridge at Musselburgh (344728) and a ford further south to deploy on the more level ground east of the river, around the village of Inveresk, which suited the English cavalry and gave a clear field of fire for Somerset's artillery. One explanation for this rash move is that Arran believed that instead of advancing, the English were moving down to their fleet with the intention of embarking, and he hoped to cut them off. More probably, Arran did not want Somerset to capture Inveresk hill. His decision was disputed by the other Scottish leaders; Angus almost mutinied, but Arran had his way and it was to cost the Scots dearly.

As the Scots moved forward, Angus was in the vanguard with a schiltron of infantrymen, a dense mass of pikemen bristling like a porcupine. Somerset sent Lord Grey forward with the heavy cavalry to charge them but the move was nearly disastrous. The Scots stood firm and Grey's men, slowed down by boggy ground in front of the Scots line, could make no impression on the rows of long pikes and suffered heavily, Grey himself being wounded. At this point, had Angus been more closely supported by Arran and the main body of the army, the battle might have taken a different turn. However, the temporary defeat of the English cavalry was checked by the Spanish mercenary captain Gamboa with a group of mounted carabineers, and by archers and hackbutters on foot who opened fire on the pikemen from a safe distance. When the Enlgish artillery began to fire on them as well, the Scots began to fall back, at first in good order. Meanwhile the left wing of the Scots, composed of Highlanders under the Earl of Argyll, moving too close to the shore, had come under fire from the fleet anchored at the mouth of the Esk and, having suffered heavy casualties, began to pull back.

At this stage the battle was still finely poised but the lack of organisation of the Scottish army turned a temporary reverse into a disaster. As Angus retired, many of his men stayed to plunder the bodies of the English cavalrymen and then, realising that they were in danger of being cut off, ran back to join their fellows. The main body of infantry, under Arran's command, saw this and, thinking that they were in full retreat, began to panic. Some of the Highlanders, alarmed by the unfamiliar noise of the artillery, had already started to disperse and the panic became general. To make the confusion worse a sudden shower of rain reduced visibility and some of Angus' men falling back were mistaken for English troops and were attacked by Arran's infantry. As the Scottish army broke up Somerset's men pursued them; many Scots were drowned trying to cross the Esk, and overall between 10,000 and 12,000 were killed, making it one of the blackest days in Scottish history.

The site of the battlefield is still largely open although the suburbs of Musselburgh and Inveresk have encroached on parts of it. The best view is from the minor road on the crest of Fälside Hill close to the castle. On the southern edge of Inveresk where the road to Carberry crosses the main east-coast railway line (350714) the right wing of Angus' infantry stood and you can see that the ground falls gently to the south-east into a dip which is still called Howe Mire (357716). This was the marshy ground which broke up Lord Grey's cavalry charge.

The Siege of Haddington, 1548-49

During the early campaigns of the 'Rough Wooing' in 1544 and 1545 Hertford's army had cut a swathe of destruction from the Border to Edinburgh. The Scots showed remarkable resilience, however, and most of the settlements which his men burned were rebuilt within a year. It was one thing to defeat the Scots in battle but another to subdue them permanently. During campaign of 1547 which culminated in the battle of Pinkie, Hertford, now Duke of Somerset, decided that instead of further invasions with large armies it might be cheaper and more effective to establish permanent garrisons on Scottish soil to try and bring the inhabitants to heel. Accordingly, he established bases in the eastern and western borders. What was needed, however, was permanent holding points in the fertile Lothians within striking distance of the capital.

In February 1548 Lord Grey of Wilton, the governor of Berwick and the leader of the heavy cavalry at Pinkie, marched into East Lothian and captured a number of strongpoints, including Hailes Castle, Yester Castle, and the towers at Herdmanston, Nunraw, Saltoun and Waughton. He was supported by some 'assured Scots', local men such as Cockburn of Ormiston, Douglas of Longniddry, and the lairds of Coalston, Humbie, Trabroun and Whittinghame, who had Protestant leanings and supported the marriage between the infant Mary and the boy king Edward. These assured Scots were used to garrison some of the outposts with men-at-arms supplied by Grey. Grey was forced to retreat following a reverse suffered by Lord Wharton in the western Borders, and Ormiston and other 'assured' lairds had their homes burnt by the Scots in reprisal. Arran, the Scottish governor, re-took Saltoun, held by the laird of Ormiston, by a surprise attack and then destroyed Ormiston's own house, cutting down the trees around it as a further act of revenge. The house of the laird of Brunstane was not only demolished; its very stones were removed.

Grey left behind a body of men to hold and fortify Haddington, and in April he was back at the head of an army. Instead of having a small garrison Grey decided to turn Haddington into a major fortress. From this point of view the town was quite suitable, being easy to fortify and lying in the heart of fertile country with many local landowners at least partly sympathetic to the English cause. Haddington was only a long day's march from the capital, as Grey showed on 3rd June when he sent a party of troops to take Dalkeith Castle. On the 7th he devastated the country as far as the Water of Leith, within two miles of Edinburgh, burning Musselburgh and the fishing villages along the coast, cutting down trees, driving off cattle and burning the crops to cause maximum destruction. Haddington had one major disadvantage, though, which became more and more apparent; it was an inland town and could be supplied only with difficulty. In fact it required a large army to provision Haddington, which defeated the idea of its garrison taking the place of a more expensive invasion force. A coastal site which could have been supplied by the English fleet would have served better. Indeed, Somerset seems to have considered using Dunbar at one stage, providing that its castle could be taken or, alternatively, Aberlady or even Musselburgh, but these plans were never implemented.

For three months the fortification of Haddington continued without interruption while the Scots waited for help from their French allies. The defences were planned by Sir Thomas Palmer, a skilled military engineer. He and Grey considered Haddington an 'evil site' to defend as it was overlooked by high ground to the north, but Grey undertook to provide Somerset with a fortress there 'or leave my bones in defence of it'. They enclosed most of the town in a square of earth and timber ramparts with strong bastions mounting cannon at the corners.

The garrison numbered up to 2,500 men, strong enough to send raiding and foraging parties far and wide. The troops manning the defences were a motley collection of English soldiers and foreign mercenaries: Spaniards, Italians and Germans. The burgh church of St. Mary (Chapter 2) lay outside the ramparts and the garrison would probably have demolished it if they had not been interrupted by the arrival of a French army.

In the middle of June reinforcements from France landed at Leith: between 6,000 and 10,000 men under the command of the Sieur d'Esse. They were as mixed a band as the 'English' defenders of Haddington, including strong contingents of Germans and Italians. They were slow to get organised but at the end of June a Franco-Scottish force surrounded Haddington and started to besiege it, sending their cannon round by sea to Aberlady. The French established their camp at Clerkington (507727) and Lethington (515721) to the south and the Scots at the nunnery east of the town (533747).

After setting up batteries of artillery they spent a week bombarding the defences prior to making an assault. The defenders worked hard by night to repair the breaches made during the day and inflicted many casualties on their attackers. On July 6th Mary of Guise, the Queen Regent, widow of James V and mother of the infant Mary, arrived at Haddington to inspect the army. She ventured forward as far as St. Mary's church, which stood close to the ramparts, and was narrowly missed by a cannon shot which wounded several of her entourage. The following day at the Scottish camp a treaty was signed under which it was agreed that the young Mary should marry the Dauphin of France, the French agreeing to provide continuing military assistance against the English invaders in return. Although the defences were badly battered by the bombardment, the all-out assault never materialised, partly due to bickering between the French and the Scots. An English relief column was able to reinforce the garrison who repaired and even improved on the defences. The French and Scots then sat down to starve the garrison into submission.

The siege was abandoned on the arrival of the Earl of Shrewsbury with an army of 12,000 infantry and 1,800 cavalry. They stocked Haddington with supplies and strengthened the garrison, burning Dunbar to the ground in passing and building a smaller fort at Dunglass to protect their lines of communication to Haddington (Chapter 3). The siege was never fully renewed, though the Scots and French made periodic attacks on English foraging parties, and in a surprise night attack on 9th October they nearly captured the town. A more insidious enemy was at work among the garrision, though: disease. By early November many soldiers in the town were sick and barely 1000 were fit to man the walls. Living conditions in Haddington, many of whose buldings had been ruined by the bombardment, were bad. Partly because of this the English kept a low profile during the winter. The following summer a new French commander, De Thermes, arrived and began more vigorous operations against the invaders. Some supplies had evidently been getting through to Haddington via Aberlady, and to block this route De Thermes had a fort built around Luffness House (Chapter 3). The English defenders, short of supplies and weakened by sickness, were content to remain within their walls. Somerset and his commanders began to realise that they did not have the forces to maintain the garrison properly and it was decided to evacuate the town, which they did at the end of September despite French efforts to trap them.

The defences at Haddington were dismantled after the Treaty of Boulogne in 1550. Nothing is visible of them today. Because they were built of earth and timber rather than stone they were comparatively easy to remove. However, if you stand on the hill at Harperdean above the town to the north (509749) you are close to the site of one of the French batteries. The entrenchments which the besiegers made have been destroyed bu cultivation but you get a view of the old part of the burgh which is similar to the one which the French had. The English fort at Dunglass (763718) and the French one at Luffness (476805) (Chapter 3) have left more traces and are worth exploring.

Mary, Queen of Scots and the Débâcle on Carberry Hill, 15th June 1567 (374696)

Only twenty years after the battle of Pinkie and barely 2km away from the battlefield a very different confrontation took place on Carberry Hill between Mary, Queen of Scots, and the Confederate Lords who opposed her marriage to the Earl of Bothwell. Bothwell had been implicated in the murder of Mary's husband, Darnley, and although officially cleared of these charges, suspicion of his involvement in the plot was still rife. Bothwell responded by abducting Mary on 24th April while she was travelling from Linlithgow to Edinburgh and carrying her off to his castle at Dunbar on the grounds that she was in danger. There are indications, however, that Mary may have been party to the plot, as the laird of Ormiston, one of Bothwell's men, is thought to have visited her secretly at Linlithgow the night before the abduction. At Dunbar, Bothwell forced Mary to agree to marry him. After three weeks they returned to Edinburgh and, after Bothwell's existing marriage was hastily dissolved, the wedding took place on 15th May. Throughout this period Mary seems to have been virtually Bothwell's prisoner and opposition to his near-dictatorship grew rapidly. On 6th June Bothwell removed Mary to Borthwick Castle south of Edinburgh for safety, but after they were besieged there he and then Mary slipped away and escaped back to Dunbar. There they began to gather supporters to challenge the rebel lords who held Mary's baby son, James.

On 14th June they left Dunbar with a small force of 60 cavalry and 200 hackbutters. As they matched through East Lothian, the strength of Bothwell's influence caused many local lairds such as Ormiston, Waughton and Lauder of the Bass to join them, as well as nobles like Lords Seton and Yester, so that they soon had an army of nearly 2,000. They halted for the night at Seton Palace and the next day marched towards Edinburgh, stopping on the commanding height of the Carberry Hill within some earthworks which had been thrown up by Somerset's forces on the eve of the battle of Pinkie. The Confederate Lords, led by the sly Earl of Morton, marched from Edinburgh early that morning under a banner bearing the device of a tree with the corpse of Darnley below and the infant James kneeling alongside with the inscription 'Judge and avenge my cause, O Lord'.

The Confederate Lords advanced to the foot of the hill and then employed the French ambassador as a mediator, with little result. The rebel nobles protested that they had no quarrel with the Queen but that they wanted the traitor who had murdered her husband. Bothwell challenged anyone who accused him of the murder to single combat. James Murray of Tullibardine accepted but Bothwell refused to fight with someone of such inferior rank and suggested Morton as a more worthy opponent. If Morton was prepared to fight, he was overruled by Lord Lindsay of the Byres who, as a relation of Darnley's, claimed precedence. Alternatively, the scheming Morton may have sub-contracted the combat! Lindsay and Bothwell were arming themselves when Mary intervened and forbade them to fight.

Meanwhile Mary's army was quietly melting away: the Confederate Lords may indeed have been spinning out the negotiations in the hope of this happening. Mary implored her troops to advance but they were reluctant to comply. When Kirkcaldy of Grange was seen advancing round the base of the hill with a body of men, as if to cut them off from Dunbar, there was a general panic and flight which left Mary with only a few supporters. She was forced to reach a compromise with her opponents, agreeing to place herself in their hands if they returned to their allegiance, and allowed Bothwell to ride off unmolested back to Dunbar. The Confederate Lords wasted no time in breaking their promises. Mary was imprisoned in Lochleven Castle, and on 24th July she gave up the throne in favour of her son who was crowned five days later. All that was left for Mary was imprisonment, a brief escape and another defeat at Langside, flight to England, further imprisonment and eventual execution. Bothwell fared no better. From Dunbar he escaped to Norway but was arrested for a previous breach of promise of marriage and died in prison.

Today the summit of Carberry Hill is still open and on the B6414 you can approach close to the site where Mary and Bothwell stood in the midst of their fickle supporters. A site on the crest of the hill, near the corner of the policies of Carberry

House, is still known as Queen Mary's Mount (374696) and may well be the position from which she saw her army, and her hopes, fade away. The mound itself, and other earthworks a short way to the south-west, are probably the remains of defences thrown up by the English army when it occupied the ridge before the battle of Pinkie.

The Battle of Dunbar, 3rd September 1650 (696767)

After the execution of Charles I in London in 1649 the Scots proclaimed his son Charles king in June 1650 he landed in Scotland. Cromwell marched north with an army to forestall the planned Scottish invasion of England. He came with about 16,000 men, battle-hardened veterans of the New Model Army, but was opposed by a larger force of up to 22,000 commanded by David Leslie. Leslie was an experienced soldier who had served under Gustavus Adolphus of Sweden. He had led the cavalry charge at Marston Moor in 1644 which contributed to the Parliamentary victory, and had beaten the renowned Marquis of Montrose at Philiphaugh the following year.

In some ways the battle was a repetition of the situation in 1547: the Scots had the larger army but their men were less well trained. Leslie fought a masterly delaying campaign, avoiding direct conflict with Cromwell but preventing him from moving through the Lothians to capture Edinburgh, and burning the crops to keep his men short of rations. He accomplished this despite having some of his best soldiers purged from the army by a committee of Covenanting ministers who did not consider their religious fervour to be sufficiently great. Cromwell was eventually forced to fall back on Dunbar where he could keep in contact with his fleet. Leslie, following him, took up station on the slopes of Doon Hill at the site still marked as 'General Leslie's Camp' by the Ordnance Survey (684754). From this exposed vantage point, despite the discomfort of wet and windy autumn weather, he could keep Cromwell's army, short of supplies and badly affected by sickness, penned up in Dunbar. If they moved towards Edinburgh or tried to retreat to Berwick he could intercept them. Few commanders could boast of having forced a general like Cromwell into such a desperate position!

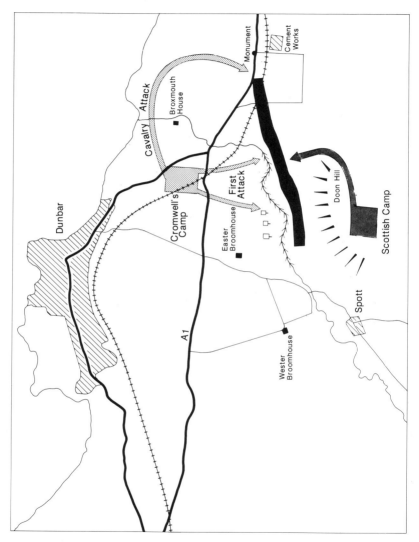

Map 8. The Battle of Dunbar, 1650.

Unfortunately for the Scots, Leslie was not his own boss. The committee of ministers, who had little knowledge of tactics, wanted to ensure that Cromwell did not escape punishment and were doubtless tired of Leslie's patient waiting game. They overruled him and forced him to move his army down to the lower northern slopes of Doon Hill where the steep valley of the Spott Burn separated them from Cromwell's troops and protected their front. An incredulous Cromwell exclaimed that the Lord had delivered them into his hands. This was the opportunity that he had been hoping for. The left wing of the Scottish army stood south of Easter Broomhouse farm at about 680762 and the right wing close to the modern AI road near the cement works at 705768. There they camped on the night of the 9th, a night of wind and rain, certain that Cromwell would not attack in such foul weather. Cromwell had, however, reconnoitred the new Scottish position from his headquarters at Broxmouth House (696777). A hillock near the house which he is supposed to have used as a vantage point is still known as 'Cromwell's Mount'. He determined on a dawn attack. While the Scottish left was well protected by the valley in front of it, the right wing was camped on more open ground which offered him greater scope for deploying his cavalry.

Before dawn Cromwell's artillery, placed to the east of Easter Broomhouse farm, opened fire on the centre of the Scottish line. A brigade of cavalry and two infantry regiments moved forward to attack Leslie's centre. If the Scots were surprised at the dawn attack they nevertheless fought well and Cromwell's forces only just managed to hold the ground they had gained south of the Spott Burn. A Scottish counter-attack forced them back a little but the Scots in turn were halted with a fresh attack by Monk on the centre of the Scottish line. The two armies were then locked in close combat for nearly two hours without either side gaining any advantage. During this period, however, Cromwell had moved his cavalry round in a wide circle north of Broxmouth House to bring them crashing into the exposed Scottish right wing. When his infantry advanced in support of the cavalry the Scottish army began to disintegrate, the right wing first and then the centre. Leslie managed to escape westwards with most of the cavalry and some of the infantry but they left behind some 3,000 dead and 10,000 prisoners, some of whom were treated extremely harshly.

A monument to the battle stands beside the A1 near the entrance to the cement works close to the position of Leslie's right wing where Cromwell's cavalry charge came smashing in. The stone bears an inscription by Thomas Carlyle and the battle cries of the two armies: 'The Covenant' for the Scots and 'The Lord of Hosts' for the English. The best position from which to view the battlefield is from the summit of Doon Hill (685757) which can be reached by a short, steep climb from a track west of Little Pinkerton farm. If you would like a less energetic walk, you can follow the road south from Easter Broomhouse to Spott to the point at which it reaches the edge of the Spott Burn (678762) and walk along the edge of the wooded valley on each side of which the armies clashed.

The Siege of the Bass Rock, June 1691-April 1694 (602873)

The most bizarre siege in the history of East Lothian was that of the Bass Rock. The island, famous for its gannet colony (Chapter 1), had a castle on it in the early fifteenth century. The rock is inaccessible on all sides save the south, facing North Berwick, where a steep rocky slope runs down to the sea and a landing can be made. In 1671 the Bass was bought by the Crown and became a state prison, being used to house various covenanting ministers, the most notable being John Blackadder, minister of Traquair, who died here.

In 1691 four young Jacobite officers who had been captured after the rout at Cromdale were sent to the Bass and were guarded by a garrison of nearly fifty men. The single landing place immediately below the castle is approachable only by small boats and is still difficult of access unless the sea is calm. The prisoners noted that when supply vessels called, most of the garrison were involved in landing the provisions. It so happened that on one occasion a boat arrived with a load of coal when the governor of the castle and many of the garrison were ashore on the mainland so that every remaining member of the prison guard had to turn out to help unload the fuel. The prisoners seized this opportunity to shut the gates on the garrison and train the castle's guns on them. Completely overlooked by the ramparts of the castle, the guards had no option but to retreat to the mainland!

The four Jacobites were later joined by a boatload of sympathisers, but at no time did the defenders number more than about twenty. Despite this they held out for nearly three years, leading a semi-piratical existence. The French government sent a warship which provisioned them, and with the aid of boats left by the vessel they were able to attack and plunder merchant ships which strayed too close to the island. They raided the coasts as far away as the Tay. Attempts were made to attack them but all efforts at bombardment from the sea failed despite the fact that the Bass Castle was not particularly strong. On one occasion a man called Trotter, who had been caught trying to run provisions to the Bass, was ordered to be hanged in sight of the island as an example. A cannon shot from the castle broke up the gathering and the execution was quickly moved out of range! The garrison only capitulated when they eventually ran out of food. When the commissioners who were negotiating the surrender visited the island the defenders used the last of their provisions to give them a lavish meal, convincing them that they had enough supplies to hold out indefinitely. As a result of this they were able to surrender on the most favourable of terms as the government despaired of getting rid of them by any other means.

Today the Bass Rock can be visited in summer by boats from North Berwick and sometimes, by prior arrangement, a landing can be made. The castle is badly ruined, having been dismantled after the siege, but it is still imposing. It consists of a curtain wall running roughly east to west across the only accessible side of the island. Cannon were mounted on the parapet above the wall and there is an angular battery at the western end. A cross-wall runs at right angles to the main curtain wall, enclosing the landing area and terminating in a half-moon battery with a low chamber pierced with gun ports below. The governor's house stood at the eastern end of the curtain wall on the site now occupied by the lighthouse.

The Battle of Prestonpans, 21st September 1745 (4074)

The west of the county was the setting for the first major Jacobite victory during the rebellion of 1745. The battlefield lies on the east side of Prestonpans. Follow the A198 south of the town to where a minor road leads off to the north at 406743.

At the time of the battle the two armies were drawn up roughly parallel to this minor road, the Hanoverian forces close to it on the west side, the Jacobites further to the east approximately where the farm of Seton West Mains stands (407747). The Hanoverian right and Jacobite left wings ended at a marshy area where the A198 runs today. The northern part of the battlefield towards Cockenzie is covered by a power station, and to the west much of the area over which the pursuit took place after the battle is a housing estate. However, the ground at the junction of the A918 and the road to Cockenzie is still open and under cultivation as it was in 1745. From here you can appreciate the topography of the area and how it influenced both the battle and the preliminary manoeuvring of the two armies.

After eluding Sir John Cope's forces in the Highlands, Prince Charles had marched south unopposed and had captured Edinburgh. Cope embarked his troops at Aberdeen and sailed south intending to land at Leith. He was not in time to save the capital and contrary winds forced him to disembark at Dunbar. His army numbered only about 2,200 men, the core of it being the infantry regiments which he had marched through the Highlands in an unsuccessful attempt to bring the Jacobites to battle and crush the rising in its early stages. These troops, who had never been under fire, were weary and demoralised after their long, fruitless journey. The dragoons accompanying them were, if anything, even less impressive. Some of them, left by Cope to guard the bridge at Stirling, had progressively fallen back as the Jacobite army approached and had panicked and fled disgracefully in full view of the citizens of Edinburgh when the Highlanders approached the capital. Colonel Gardiner, who commanded one of the dragoon

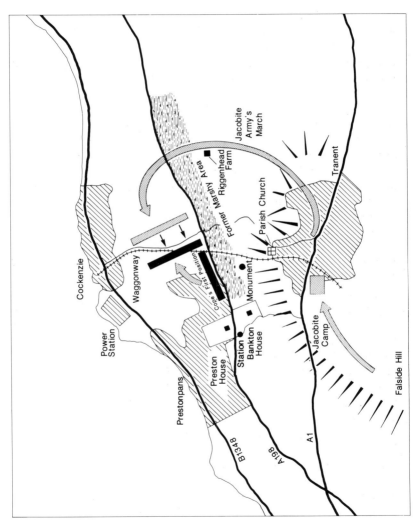

Map 9. The Battle of Prestonpans, 1745.

Prince Charles Edward Stuart, victor of the battle of Prestonpans in 1745.

regiments, privately admitted that, when it came to the crunch, he doubted if more than ten of his men would follow him in a charge under fire. Cope also had six small field guns and some mortars but no proper gunners, only a few elderly soldiers supported by some seamen borrowed from the naval vessels which had brought him to Dunbar.

On Thursday 19th September Cope set out for Edinburgh. Camping overnight west of Haddington, he pushed on along the main post road towards Tranent. Having no firm indications of the movements of the Jacobites, he descended towards the coast where the ground was more open. Meanwhile, the Jacobite army had left their camp at Duddingston, south-east of Edinburgh, on the 20th and marched towards Musselburgh. Prince Charles' army amounted to around 2,000 men, the bulk of them Highlanders grouped into clan regiments of varying sizes. Perhaps three quarters were armed with broadswords and a miscellany of firearms from muskets to fowling-pieces but some had only improvised weapons including scythe blades mounted on poles. The Jacobites had no cavalry worth mentioning and no artillery at all. While the two armies were virtually equal in size Cope, who had received little intelligece concerning his opponents, believed that their forces greatly outnumbered his own and his cautious tactics were based on this assumption.

Once across the River Esk, Jacobite scouts observed Cope's forward patrols of dragoons near the village of Preston. Believing that Cope would try to gain the commanding ridge of Falside Hill, south-west of Tranent (382714), Lord George Murray pushed forward to reach it. Cope, however, on being warned of the enemy's approach, stood fast of a level site east of Preston. Superficially the Jacobites held a strong position overlooking Cope's army but the detail of the topography gave the advantage to the Hanoverians. Cope has been pilloried as a blundering, incompetent soldier but his choice of ground was eminently sensible. Wheeling his forces to the south to face the Jacobites, his front was protected by a marshy area drained by a series of ditches, the largest of which presented a major obstacle to an attacking force. His right was protected by high stone walls around Preston House (392739) and Bankton House (395737), the home of Colonel Gardiner the dragoon commander. The marsh protecting Cope's front was crossed by a colliery tramway whose line can still be followed from Tranent at 403730 down a steep gully called The Heugh towards the sea at Cockenzie (Chapter 10), but this narrow access way was easily blocked. In addition to this protection, Cope had drawn his army up on dry level ground which should have allowed him to deploy his cavalry and artillery to best advantage.

The Jacobites spent the afternoon and evening of the 20th trying to find a way to get at their opponents. At first, the Highlanders were stationed west of Tranent in case Cope should try and slip past towards Edinburgh. A party of Camerons had been posted in the churchyard at 403734 overlooking the Hanoverian right. After discovering them, Cope had two of his cannon brought up, the fire from which dislodged them. The Jacobite commander Lord George

Murray decided that the only feasible direction to attack was from the east but this would have involved a long, difficult detour around the marsh. However, Robert Anderson, the son of a local laird, came forward and offered to guide the Jacobites through the marsh by a more direct path. They set off at about 4a.m. following a route north from Tranent to the farm of Riggonhead (416743) and from there north-westwards through the marsh. The noise of their passage alerted Cope's patrols and he had just enough time to reform his army at right angles to its original position, facing east. After passing through the marsh the Jacobites formed up facing the Hanoverian line, darkness and then early morning mist hiding their activities until the last moment.

Cope drew his regiments up three deep with his guns and mortars on the extreme right. They might have been better in the centre but there was no time to move them. Most of his dragoons were on the flanks with two squadrons in reserve. The Jacobites attacked at sunrise advancing at a fast run. This unnerved the gunners who turned and fled. Two of their officers managed to fire off most of the pieces, causing the advancing Highlanders to check momentarily, but without gun crews there was no chance of reloading. The dragoons on Cope's right, ordered to advance and take the Highlanders in the flank, came to within pistol shot but began to turn and retreat after receiving the first musket shots from the Highlanders. Panic was infectious, spreading first to the artillery guard who began to edge backwards. The dragoons on the left wing also panicked and galloped back out of range. Deserted by the cavalry, the infantry who formed the main part of Cope's line were left to bear the brunt of the attack. Their thin line began to waver. They fired a single un-coordinated volley of musketry whose effect was limited. After firing at the run the Highlanders threw their muskets away and came on with their broadswords. The Hanoverian line was pierced in several places by dense bodies of clansmen, and despite frantic efforts by Cope and his officers to rally the infantry they disintegrated and a total rout ensued.

Many of the fleeing infantry were trapped against the stone walls around Preston House and were cut down by broadswords, Lochaber axes, or scythe blades before the

Jacobite officers could restrain their men. Colonel Gardiner, abandoned by his dragoons, was mortally wounded in sight of his home while trying to rally some of the infantry. He was carried to the manse at Tranent where he died, and he was buried at the west end of the parish church.

Sir John Cope formed up a body of panic-stricken dragoons near Preston village and, realising that nothing would persuade them to attack, led them off southwards by a road which today runs from Prestonpans station (393738) to the west end of Tranent (394730) and is still called 'Johnnie Cope's Road'.

This recalls the scurrilous Jacobite song, 'Hey Johnnie Cope', by Adam Skirving, a local Jacobite sympathiser, which portrays the Hanoverian commander as arrogant and overconfident:

> Cope sent a challenge frae Dunbar
> Saying Charlie meet me, an' ye daur
> And I'll teach ye the art of war
> If ye'll meet me in battle in the morning.

Cope then retreated across the hills to Berwick although, contrary to the words of the song, he did not actually bring the first news of his own defeat! Some 300 of the Hanoverian army were killed and about 1,500 – virtually all the surviving infantry – captured, while the Jacobites claimed to have lost about thirty men in the battle.

Today the marshy ground has mostly been drained but traces of the ditch which protected Cope's original front line can be seen beside the A198. The best view of the battlefield is from the parish church of Tranent (402735). Much of the battlefield is still open but the site has changed a lot. The view is dominated by the power station at Cockenzie, criss-crossed by lines of electricity pylons, cut by the new by-pass in the foreground and partly built over by a housing estate. The line of the waggonway can still be followed down the hill from Tranent. It runs below the church and has been landscaped to make an attractive walk. The most evocative site associated with the battle is undoubtedly Colonel Gardiner's house at Bankton. It stands behind a farmyard just south of Prestonpans station, a roofless shell at one end of an overgrown avenue of trees which leads to a monument erected in the nineteenth century to the colonel's memory.

CHAPTER 5
The Changing Countryside

Much of the East Lothian countryside is comparatively recent in date, the creation of the revolution in agriculture and rural life during the later eighteenth and early nineteenth centuries. The new landscape with its regular fields, neat hedges, and large farm steadings swept away much of the pre-existing landscape within a couple of generations. Some features of the pre-improvement landscape such as castles and mansions, churches and chapels are dealt with in other chapters but here we are concerned with how the landscape of fields, pastures and woodlands around them evolved into the modern countryside.

The Countryside before the Improvers

If we had a time machine to take us back to East Lothian in the sixteenth, seventeenth or early eighteenth centuries, what would the countryside have looked like? We have enough indications from travellers' reports, topographers' descriptions and more mundane estate records to have a good idea. If we could be transported back in time and set down on a suitable vantage point like Traprain Law or the Garleton Hills, one of the first features that would probably strike us would be the absence of woodland. Millennia of forest clearance with little or no replanting, and periodic devastation like the campaigns of the 1540s, meant that East Lothian, like most parts of the Scottish Lowlands, was virtually treeless. Another feature which would strike us would be the lack of field boundaries and enclosures. Instead of the neatly parcelled-out landscape we see today with its sharply-defined geometrical boundaries we would see an open landscape in which a patchwork of greens, yellows and browns were subtly merged. The only trees and enclosures would have been the policies around the castles and mansions of the landowners, and these were of limited extent before the mid-eighteenth century. Nevertheless, they made

John Slezer's view of Haddington in the 1690s. Note the ridge and furrow in the open fields in the foreground.

the mansions stand out like islands in a sea of open land, emphasising the dominance of their owners over the rural population.

The arable land was still open and unenclosed, the holdings worked by the tenants in each village and farm being intermingled in strips and blocks in a system known as 'runrig' which was designed to give every farmer a share of the best and worst land in a township. The arable land was divided into the infield and the outfield. The infield was cultivated intensively with an endless succession of cereal crops: mainly oats and bere (a hardy form of barley) with wheat on the best soils. Crops of peas and beans were often taken between the cereals as farmers were aware that legumes improved soil fertility although they had no idea how this happened. Fallow on the infield, to give it a rest between cereal crops, was virtually unknown. Continuous cultivation was maintained by the application of large quantities of animal manure supplemented along the coast by seaweed and around the towns by stable litter and other refuse. The outfield was only cropped with oats, the hardiest cereal, for the sole manure which this land received was dung from cattle folded on parts of it inside temporary turf dykes during the summer. The land was soon worn out and was left to recover for a few years before being ploughed up once more. There were no permanent boundaries within the open fields. Although this was a fertile and well-tilled area compared with most parts of Scotland, a surprising amount of land was uncultivated at any time, in permanent rough pasture, natural hay meadow to provide winter fodder, or outfield lying fallow. The livestock were taken away from the arable land during the summer, up to the hill pastures or to areas of rough grazing known as 'commonties' which were shared between different landowners.

Abandoned Fields and Farmsteads

The only vestige of these old field systems which can be seen today lie in the Lammermuirs. In the past, with a fairly primitive agricultural technology, it was often easier to cultivate well-drained slopes, even at high altitudes, than to drain more level but marshy land in the valleys. If you look at the hillsides and higher valleys in the Lammermuirs, above the limits of modern cultivation and improved pasture, you can often see traces of ridges under the grass or heather, running parallel, roughly downslope and up to five or six metres wide. This is 'ridge and furrow', evidence of ploughing from the days before underground tile drains became the normal way of draining fields. The ridges were thrown up by ploughing the land in strips, starting from the middle and working to the margins, the plough always throwing the furrow slice towards the centre so that over time the centre of the strip became humped – the ridge – and the edges low – the furrow. This was done deliberately to help drainage; water was shed from the ridges into the furrows and then ran downslope into larger field drains.

Where the ridges are less uniform and tend to curve, the field patterns are older. These less regular ridges may date from medieval times but can be as recent as the eighteenth century as methods of ploughing do not seem to have changed much over this period. If you are passing through the Lammermuirs, particularly down the valleys of the Whiteadder and its tributaries, or are walking over the hills between them, look out for traces of ridge and furrow, along with the boundaries, access ways and settlements which adjoined them.

These ancient fields are often brought out by differences in vegetation between the drier ridges and wetter furrows, or stand out in shadows with low-slanting sunlight early in the morning or in the evening.

One reason why land at such high altitudes – up to nearly 400m in places – was cultivated in medieval times was that the climate was drier and milder then than at any period since. This allowed a growing population to expand on to marginal land whose cultivation ceased to be feasible in later centuries. Many of these small, pioneer holdings were bought out by the great monastic estates who turned much of the uplands into great sheep ranges based on communal farms or 'granges' (Chapter 2). The fall of population after the Black Death may also have encouraged the abandonment of these high-lying holdings on soils which were thin and poor. Another more insidious enemy may have been the climate. From the fourteenth century, culminating in the later seventeenth century, the climate became colder and wetter, driving the limits of cultivation downhill and encouraging the abandonment of these high-lying fields, and the settlements which were associated with them. Despite this retreat levels of cultivation shown on the Military Survey of 1747-55 were still far higher than would be considered worthwhile today. During the second half of the eighteenth century a process of rationalisation was adopted by which large areas of high-lying land were abandoned and much uncultivated ground at lower altitudes was brought under the plough.

Old documents and maps make it possible to establish roughly when some of these remote steadings were abandoned. One nameless farm and its fields on the edge of the hills south of Spott (669715) seem to have been abandoned before 1600, as was a site on the Kilmade Burn near the Whiteadder reservoir (665628). Other farms went out of use during the seventeenth and early eighteenth centuries, possibly because of the harsher climate. Examples are Birkcleuch (678665) and Knowis (671663) beside the Bothwell Water and Cribbes (709663) on the Monynut Water.

Not all ridge and furrow is ancient, though. Where the ridges are very regular and straight they were often created during the Napoleonic Wars when rising grain prices encouraged farmers to plough high-lying ground which they would never have contemplated cultivating under normal conditions. Much of this land was abandoned soon after Waterloo! The former fields around the old castle of Gamelshiel high in the Lammermuirs (650647) are an example. The remote farm of Darned House (603662) at the head of an empty valley under the appropriately named Bleak Law was abandoned even later, during the mid-nineteenth century.

Doos and Doocots

Although much of the old rural landscape of East Lothian was swept away during the eighteenth and nineteenth centuries, one feature which typifies the old order in the countryside has survived in substantial numbers: the doocot. Doocots were a perquisite of landed proprietors, and one reason why so many remain in this area is that it was a country of small, though wealthy, estates with plenty of good arable land. Another reason for their survival may be the old tradition that ill luck was liable to befall anyone who demolished a doocot. Pigeons were a valuable source of fresh meat during winter, a change from the flesh of cattle which were slaughtered and salted at Martinmas. However, pigeons made great inroads on grain in the surrounding fields. While a statute of 1503 had encouraged landowners to build doocots as sources of food, an act of the Scottish Parliament in 1617 restricted their construction. Under this act they could only be erected for proprietors who had a rent income of ten chalders of grain drawn from lands within two miles of the proposed doocot. The idea was that the birds would feed mainly at the expense of the landowner's own tenants rather than that of his neighbours!

Doocots were simply stone structures with hundreds of ledges inside for the birds to nest on and a hole for them to fly in and out. Nevertheless, variations in their design are a study in themselves. The oldest surviving ones were built during the sixteenth century: one at Athelstaneford (533734) has a date of 1583 on it, another at Tranent 1587 (403734). These early doocots are of two types. The first is the beehive-shape, circular in section and tapering towards the top like fat pepperpots.

A good example of a circular doocot in Preston village with the roofs of Northfield House in the background.

They often have protruding string courses or stone ledges running around the outside to prevent rats from climbing in and destroying the eggs. Good examples of beehive-shaped doocots can be found at Dirleton Castle (515839), Phantassie near Preston Mill (597774) and two in the village of Preston (389739).

The other early style is a rectangular type known as a lectern because of its sloping top. The one at Athelstaneford is of this type, and some double lectern doocots also exist as at Letham House near Haddington (494734). Doocots usually face south to give the birds a sunny surface to sit on while sheltering them from cold northerly winds. Doocots continued to be built well into the eighteenth century and have a variety of decorations from crow-stepped gables to classical columns and pediments. Later ones are often round like the one attached to the farm opposite the church at Bolton (506701) or Lady Kitty's doocot beside the Nungate Bridge in Haddington. The smallest doocots could usually accommodate about 500 birds but one of the largest, at Johnstounburn (461608), could house some

2,000 pigeons. This doocot is unusual in having a central pillar lined with nesting boxes in addition to those built into the inside of the walls. Many doocots still adjoin estate mansions and are not readily accessible, but if you would like to see the interior of one, the National Trust for Scotland owns the doocot at Phantassie, next to Preston Mill (597774), and you can go inside and examine the nesting boxes and the ladders giving access to the various levels. While you are holding your noses against the smell, you might like to reflect that pigeon droppings, periodically cleared out of the bottoms of doocots, were the most highly prized manure available! It is also possible to get a key for the doocot at Northfield in Preston village from the nearby cottages. Other doocots with public access include the one in Lady Kitty's Garden in Haddington, near St. Mary's Church (518737), and the double lectern one at Tantallon Castle (595850) which has 1200 nesting boxes.

Planting; Parks and Policies

During the seventeenth and early eighteenth centuries the countryside was not static though change was slow. Along with the extension and improvement of East Lothian country houses in the later seventeenth century the fashion for extending and embellishing the surrounding policies developed. This involved enclosing them into parks and planting woodlands. The mains or home farm was often enclosed at the same time and proprietors tentatively introduced new agricultural techniques. They fattened cattle in their parks and imported English breeding stock to improve their own animals. They also tried new crop rotations. This fashion was assisted by an act of the Scottish Parliament in 1661 which offered tax relief on land enclosed in this way.

One of the earliest of these parks was at Lethington (now Lennoxlove – 515721) in 1681 by the Duke of Lauderdale. The story is that Lauderdale built it for a visit to Scotland by the Duke of York (later James VII). On a previous trip to Scotland James had claimed that there were not 400 acres enclosed in all of Scotland; Lauderdale, determined to prove otherwise, had 400 acres surrounded by a stone wall nearly 4m high! The outline of the park is still traceable as a rough quadrilateral centred on Lennoxlove House, bounded by the A6137 and B6369 roads.

John Hay, the second earl of Tweeddale, was already creating an extensive park at Yester to ornament a new house which was never started in his lifetime. The policies at Yester were probably the largest in Scotland at that time, extending to over 1000 acres. A description of the plantations there, written about 1720, stated that the perimeter wall was eight miles in circumference and protected a million mature trees. This is probably an exaggeration but the scale of planting was undoubtedly unique in Scotland at that period. The impact of these attempts to beautify the surroundings of East Lothian's country houses is shown dramatically on John Adair's map of East Lothian, drawn in the 1690s, which marks the new plantations as islands of woodland in a sea of open-field cultivation. A striking legacy of this activity is the high stone policy walls which, given the density of estates in the county, are notable wherever you go.

Perhaps the most famous early improver was Thomas, sixth earl of Haddington, whose estate was at Tyninghame. From about 1706 he began to lay out plantations and enclosures, often on sandy coastal soils which his neighbours thought too poor to be worth the effort. He placed shelter belts of trees around his enclosures to protect them from the sea winds but he also planted large blocks of woodland. The 400-acre Binning Wood (600800) and other neighbouring woodlands were celebrated throughout Scotland, particularly as they contained lots of beech trees which until that time had been rare north of the Border. The woods were not merely ornamental; they were also big business. The earl of Haddington received an annual income of some £500 sterling for the thinnings alone and later, when the trees were mature, a sawmilling industry developed at Tyninghame. The earl was also one of the first East Lothian landowners to experiment with fallowing his arable land between cereal crops and to try clover and sown grasses as crops, to the scorn of neighbouring farmers who could not see the sense of sowing grass on land that could have produced a crop of corn.

The plantations on the earl of Haddington's estate are the largest in the lowland part of the county. This is partly because most of the land was too fertile to be used in this way but also because some coastal areas are too exposed for trees to thrive. You can see this along the coast road between Longniddry and Aberlady (443775). The trees inside the policy wall around Gosford house sweep back sharply at an angle from the top of the wall showing the effects of the prevailing westerly winds and emphasising the need for shelter. Other houses with attractive parks and plantations are Biel (637759) and Broxmouth (697776), near Dunbar, and Archerfield (505841) near Dirleton, where the soils are thin and sandy like those at Tyninghame.

Much of the lowland part of the county is still open with little woodland. It is south of the Tyne towards the edge of the Lammermuirs that you find more extensive plantations, partly because the soils are poorer here and the topography more varied, with steeper slopes which are unfit for farming but suitable for afforestation. It was here, in the early 1740s, slightly later that the Earl of Haddington's pioneer work, that the Marquis of Tweeddale began to enclose land on his estates at Yester using beech hedges. After his death the hedges were left without proper maintenance and many grew into closely-spaced mature trees. Some of these tall beech hedges can still be seen around Gifford, and some well-maintained ones fringe the A6137 road near Cauldshiel (490652).

The first East Lothian landowner to set about remodelling his entire estate, rather than just the parklands around his house, was John Cockburn of Ormiston. His father, Adam Cockburn, had made a start but it was left to John to see the process through. Cockburn was an ardent Anglophile, a supporter of the Union of 1707 who sat as member for Haddington in the new Westminster Parliament. His close contact with England had made him aware of the backward state of Scottish agriculture and he resolved to imitate English practices on his own estate when he succeeded to it in 1714. He began granting long leases on favourable terms to some of his tenants if they agreed to start enclosing their farms with hedges and ditches. He commenced with four farms on relatively poor soils south of the River Tyne: Dodridge (418649), House o'

Another doocot in Preston village, this time in a lectern style.

Muir (415669), Murrays (412662) and West Byres (408674) which were soon enclosed, and had the steadings of these and other farms rebuilt on more efficient lines.

Cockburn also rebuilt the village of Ormiston as a model community with the aid of an English land surveyor (see Chapter 7). He founded an agricultural society at Ormiston for local landowners and tenants who met monthly to discuss improvements in farming. He also promoted industry on his estate, particularly linen manufacture, bringing in workers from Ireland and Holland to teach the local inhabitants the best ways to prepare flax and setting up a school for young girls to learn spinning. Cockburn tried to encourage changes for social rather than purely profit-making reasons and the economic climate was not sufficiently favourable for his efforts to succeed. He went bankrupt, selling out to the Earl of Hopetoun in 1747. However, his work had attracted widespread interest – other East Lothian landowners had sent their best tenants to Ormiston to learn the new techniques which Cockburn was practising, and the best of his own farmers went on to make names for themselves as improvers in their own right.

The 'Agricultural Revolution'

Although changes in agriculture began earlier in East Lothian than in other parts of Scotland, progress only accelerated from the 1760s, and especially during the last twenty years of the century. The most notable change in the landscape was the removal of the old infields and outfields and their replacement by the modern pattern of regular enclosed fields bounded by hedges or stone walls. At the same time there was a marked expansion in the area under cultivation. The old system of arable farming provided little fodder for the livestock which required large areas of rough pasture and natural hay meadow. Every farm had areas of permanent grass between the fields, and many parishes had huge common pastures, some of them in the Lammermuirs but a good deal at low level. Even the burghs had large unimproved moors on which the burgesses could graze livestock and cut peat and turf for fuel and roofing. Haddington had over 1000 acres of rough grazing in Gladsmuir parish while Dunbar had a huge expanse of pasture in the Lammermuirs which is still known as 'Dunbar Common' (6369).

The development of new crop rotations with fallow courses, sown grasses and legumes like clover produced more fodder from the arable land and cut down the need for permanent pasture. So did crops of turnips which could be fed to sheep in the fields and to cattle in enclosed courts at the new farm steadings. This allowed the commons to be ploughed up and enclosed. Large areas of low-lying moorland were removed in this way, the land being annexed to existing farms or new ones established. When you travel through East Lothian in winter and see sheep feeding on turnips in the fields you are looking at a scene which epitomises the Agricultural Revolution and the changes in the landscape which accompanied it. The enclosures were fenced off by hawthorn hedges and stone dykes. Hedges had the advantage of creating an ever more effective barrier through time when properly maintained, while dykes were never more efficient than when first built and needed increasing maintenance as they became older. Stone walls did, however, use up the large quantities of boulders which encumbered the soils and which were gradually removed from the fields to make ploughing easier. In the higher parts of the county hedges did not thrive in exposed conditions and stone walls had the advantage of being more effective barriers to sheep.

Although improvements accelerated slowly during the eighteeth century, the main period of change occupied only a couple of generations after about 1760 and the transformation of the landscape was rapid. Early in the eighteenth century Cockburn of Ormiston and other East Lothian landowners were bringing in English farmers to teach their backward and conservative tenants better techniques. So thorough was the transformation that by the early nineteenth century English landowners were coming to East Lothian for instruction. The end product of these changes was a highly efficient, rationally laid-out landscape.

We tend to think of 'factory farming' as a twentieth-century phenomenon but William Cobbett, the celebrated English writer on agriculture and rural life, who visited East Lothian in the early nineteenth century, was impressed, almost overawed, by the new farming landscape which he saw: 'The land is the finest that I ever saw in my life', he commented, having already seen the most fertile parts of England; 'turnips . . . all in rows as straight as a line and without a weed ever to be seen in any of these beautiful fields . . . the farmer's house is a house big enough and fine enough for a gentleman to live in'. On another visit he commented that 'here are fields with trees round them like the finest and largest fields in Sussex and Kent . . . land as fine as it is possible to be . . . Everything is abundant here except people who have been studiously swept from the land'. Indeed, the farmlands of East Lothian do sometimes look empty because of the lack of isolated houses and cottages but Cobbett was misled by this into thinking that the land had been depopulated. In fact the big new farmsteads with their attendant cottages often held as many people as small villages elsewhere. The modern East Lothian countryside is still largely the product of this short but energetic period of change only slightly modified by more recent developments.

The New Farmsteads

The new landscape of highly commercialised farming was organised around farmsteads of improved design. There was a gradual change in the construction of farm buildings in East Lothian in the later eighteenth century towards better-built, more spacious and more efficiently laid-out ranges of outbuildings. Early illustrations and descriptions show that the old farmsteads were often laid out in a row with the barn and byre at either end of the farm house, or merely in a random scatter. As early as 1699 Lord Belhaven, the first East Lothian landowner to write a treatise on agricultural improvement, advocated a courtyard layout with the barn on the western side, aligned north-south so that a through draught from prevailing westerly winds allowed the grain and chaff to be separated by winnowing. The farmhouse, Belhaven wrote, should face south across the courtyard with the stables and byres opposite and the dunghill in the middle.

Gradually this plan was adopted during the eighteenth century so that farmsteads were laid out around a courtyard with the fourth side enclosed by a wall and later by another range of buildings incorporating a large entrance arch. Only a few examples survive of this first generation of improved farm buildings, which were constructed by local masons in a true vernacular tradition. Outside the courtyard, on the west of the barn, was the stack yard where the corn was stored before threshing, sited so that it got plenty of air to prevent the sheaves from over-heating and rotting. In the courtyard cattle were fed during the winter. With the introduction of the threshing machine (see below) the barn was modified to a T-shape. It now had a line of cart sheds facing into the courtyard, the number of arches being a good measure of the size of the farm. Above this were granaries with the threshing barn at right angles behind. The machinery for driving the threshing machine stood in the angle between the two parts of

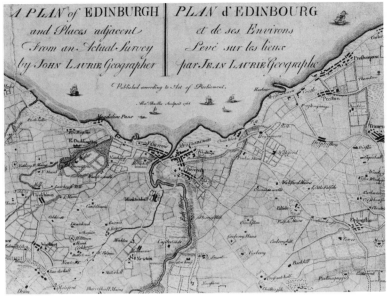

Laurie's map of 1766 shows the countryside around Musselburgh. You can see how little of the countryside had been enclosed at this period. Along the coast you can pick out industrial sites including potteries and coal mines.

the barn. On the other sides of the courtyard were byres, stables and storage space for equipment. In the earlier courtyard farms the tenant's house formed part of the complex, but the dunghill at the door did not fit well with the new 'genteel' image of the increasingly prosperous farmers. As a result the farmhouse, now an elegant two- or sometimes three-storey building, became set apart from the outbuildings, emphasising the increasing social distance between the farmer and his workers.

Most of the farmsteads which you see today date from a later phase of rebuilding from the 1820s to the 1850s with, in many cases, later alterations and additions. These nineteenth-century steadings were architect-designed and, though laid out on strictly functional lines, they were often embellished to a greater degree than their predecessors. They were built when East Lothian farming was very prosperous and farmers and landowners alike were prepared to re-invest much of their profits in their farms and outbuildings.

If you look at East Lothian farmsteads you will notice that in many cases the farmhouse is roofed with slate and the outbuildings with pantiles which, although giving many steadings an attractive warm red appearance, were not thought fit for roofing anything better than a cottage until the later nineteenth century. The pantiles were originally imported from Holland as ballast but were later made locally, becoming the standard replacement for straw thatch which had been the old roofing material for outbuildings.

In some parts of Scotland most of the farm workers were unmarried and lived in communal bothies which formed part of the outbuildings. The East Lothian practice was to employ married ploughmen. Sometimes married farm workers' cottages were incorporated into the farm courtyard, as at Saltoun Mains (465689), but mostly they were built close to, but detached from, the steading in a separate group. Rows of farm workers' cottages with pantile roofs and solid sandstone walls were the normal accompaniment of the new farmsteads and they are still prominent in the landscape. There is a particularly good example opposite the station at Drem (510796), while at Markle Mains (563776) the cottages form an attractive group in a hollow below the farmstead.

Some of the new steadings were given ornate decoration with clock towers, like Athelstaneford Mains (541771), or dovecotes surmounting the arch which led into the courtyard, as at Monkrigg Mains near Haddington (524727) or Harelaw near Longniddry (445767). At Saltoun Mains (465869), where the farm buildings occupy three sides of a courtyard with a low wall on the fourth, a polygonal dovecot tower at the rear dominates the farm. The architectural styles of these nineteenth-century farmsteads varied greatly. Some larger estates had a characteristic 'house style' of architecture which included steadings, farmhouses and labourers' cottages; it can be interesting to try and identify these. For example, steadings and other buildings on the Wemyss estate around Aberlady, many of them built in the 1830s, have a distinctive Tudor style. The farms of Craigielaw (453798) and Spittal (468772) are good examples.

Elsewhere, you can find Scottish baronial decoration with

A farmstead at Samuelston, near Haddington. The chimney stack shows that in the early 19th century this farm was prosperous enough to afford a steam-driven threshing machine.

crow-stepped gables above the entrance to the courtyard and on the wings at either end of the facade as at Kirklandhill (618779) between East Linton and Dunbar. Gothic revival architecture is a feature of Papple (591725) and Trabroun (467743), with high-pitched roofs and pointed windows and arches. Sunnyside (594795) looks like a medieval castle. Phantassie, near East Linton (598773), built about 1840, is a good example of a steading with a severe classical style as is Monkrigg Mains (525727). One of the most impressive of these great courtyard farmsteads is Greendykes, east of Tranent (437737), which was built around 1830 and was used as a model in an architect's handbook of farm and cottage designs.

Andrew Meikle and the Threshing Machine

There were few mechanical innovations associated with these changes but some of the most important were associated with the Meikle family of East Lothian millwrights. They show how local talent, with the right backing, could produce technological changes of international importance. Early in the eighteenth century James Meikle, millwright at Wester Keith, had brought from Holland the idea of a winnowing machine for separating the grain from the chaff, and also the design for a pot-barley mill. Previous to this barley being prepared for broth or ale had the husks removed by a simple 'knocking stone' or mortar and pestle. Meikle was sent to Holland in 1710 by Andrew Fletcher of Saltoun with orders to note the processes involved and, where necessary, bring back appropriate pieces of machinery to be copied in Scotland: an early example of industrial espionage! For a long time the mill on the Saltoun estate was the only one of its kind in Scotland and shops all over the country sold 'Saltoun barley'.

James Meikle's elder son Robert followed his father as a millwright but branched out into a range of industrial enterprises, mainly in the west of Scotland. He designed mills for the Duke of Argyll, the Forfeited Estates Commissioners and various private companies before moving into canal and dock schemes and other engineering ventures. He was working at a time when the profession of engineer had scarcely started to become separated from the ordinary craftsman, and as a result his work is scarcely remembered today.

More famous is James Meikle's younger son Andrew (1719-1811) who lived and worked in East Lothian throughout his life. He was miller first at Saltoun then at Houston Mill near East Linton and finally at Knowes Mill nearby. He developed the first effective machine for threshing grain. Other inventors had built prototypes before him but they were either insufficiently robust or damaged the grain. Sir Francis Kinloch of Gilmerton, near Athelstaneford, had tried to improve on previous models without success and sent his designs to Meikle. Meikle developed them further and hit on the idea of a rapidly rotating drum which shook the grain out of the corn by velocity rather than battering or rubbing it out.

He produced his first threshing machine for a farmer near Clackmannan but the second one was installed at Phantassie near East Linton, owned by George Rennie, one of the foremost improving farmers in the county. His younger brother John, who served his apprenticeship as a millwright under Andrew Meikle, was the famous engineer. Unfortunately Andrew Meikle, who died in 1811 aged 92 and

By the middle of the nineteenth century farm outbuildings were being decorated in a variety of styles. This example near Garvald has been ornamented to resemble a medieval castle.

is buried in the churchyard at Prestonkirk, did not make much money out of his invention. His patent was widely infringed and he died before a collection of £1,500, raised by Sir John Sinclair in appreciation of the importance of his work, could be presented to him. His son George Meikle kept up the family tradition and was responsible in 1787 for designing the giant water wheel at Blairdrummond near Stirling which allowed the drainage and reclamation of the great expanse of peat moss there.

Meikle's threshing machine could be driven by various means. The most common method was horse power, with two, four or sometimes six horses walking in a continuous circle within a round or polygonal building attached to the side of the barn, variously known as a horse mill, horse gin, horse gang or wheelhouse. These can still be seen on many East Lothian steadings. There is a good one at Markle Mains (574779) near East Linton, and another on the outskirts of Dunbar (685784) has been restored with an explanatory plaque. This source of power was cheap to install but it made exhausting work for the horses.

Saturday morning in North Berwick.

Other power sources were tried, including water and even wind. Water mills cost no more than horse gins but not every farm had a convenient stream nearby. At Crowhill, on the banks of the Thornton Burn (735741), the farmer was so keen to install a water-driven threshing machine that in 1812 he had a 250-foot-long shaft built in a tunnel to transmit power from the water mill to the farmstead which stood nearly twenty metres above the stream. The mill, shaft, tunnel and threshing machine house still survive. Windmill-driven threshing machines cost about twice as much as horse or water-driven ones and were liable to damage by sudden gusts of wind until the ever-resourceful Meikle invented a system for taking in the sails of such mills quickly by a rope worked from inside the mill. In the 1820s and 1830s, when steam power was being widely applied in factories, and when the roads of East Lothian had been improved sufficiently to allow coal to be brought cheaply to almost every part of the lowlands, the fashion developed for installing steam engines to drive threshing machines. The first steam threshing machine in the county was installed as early as 1803 but it took time for the idea to spread.

Above many of the larger steadings rose the tall chimneys of the steam engines and, although a number of them have been demolished in recent years for safety reasons, some can still be seen. There is a fine one at Beanston (546763), east of Athelstaneford. Other examples can be seen at Sunnyside (554755) and Luggate (596748) near Traprain Law. By the mid-1840s East Lothian had 386 threshing machines: 269 driven by horse power, 80 by steam, 30 by water and 7 by wind.

Another scene in North Berwick.

CHAPTER 6
Houses Great and Small

Much of East Lothian's character derives from its houses, ranging from the mansions of the larger landowners to the cottages which contribute so much to the attractive appearance of the county's villages. In this chapter we outline the history of East Lothian's houses, great and small, from the seventeenth century onwards. East Lothian is a county of small, though prosperous, estates. This had produced a landscape liberally dotted with country houses of all sizes ranging from small lairds' dwellings to great mansions. Chapter 3 has looked at castles and tower houses, which remained the normal dwelling for landowners into the seventeenth century. This chapter considers the houses which replaced them from the seventeenth century onwards. It then looks at the homes of the ordinary people of East Lothian, the farmers, cottagers and labourers, who made up the bulk of the population.

Only a limited number of East Lothian's country houses are open to the public but the exteriors of many others can be viewed from a little distance while it is sometimes possible to gain access to their grounds or 'policies' for a closer look. In this chapter we have concentrated, as far as possible, on describing houses which are accessible to the public to some degree, but in order to present a balanced picture we also include houses of architectural importance which may not be so easy to view. The description of any house in this chapter is, therefore, no guarantee of right of access to the building or its grounds. We have indicated in the gazetteer those houses which are regularly open to the public, but for others it is advisable to seek permission before going off a public road. As with castles and towers we have not attempted a comprehensive survey, as this would result in a mere catalogue. For full details of all East Lothian's mansions you should consult the invaluable volume on Lothian in the *Buildings of Scotland* series.

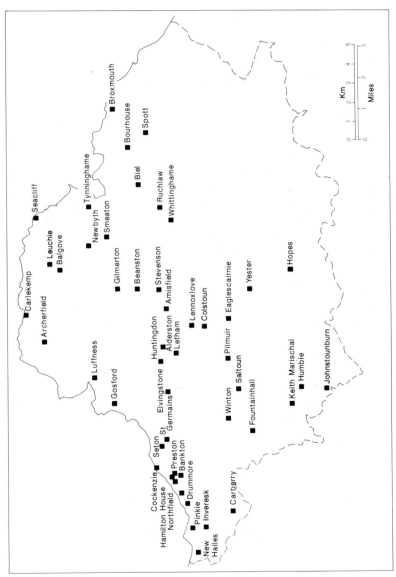

Map 10. Country Houses.

The First Undefended Mansions

In some parts of Scotland the tradition of the fortified house died slowly. Even in the early seventeenth century completely new towers and castles were being built in areas like Aberdeenshire. To be sure, they were more highly ornamented than their predecessors, with picturesque pepperpot turrets rising from their wall-heads. But they were still castles, their entrances protected by iron grilles or 'yetts' and flanked by gun loops, with windows at a safe distance above the ground. While they made some concessions to greater comfort and modernity, their owners were evidently taking no risks!

East Lothian was different, though. In the later sixteenth century the threat of invasion from south of the Border was receding. Local feuding was also fast dying out in an area which was close to the capital. From the early seventeenth century, when James VI had installed himself at Westminster and had united the two kingdoms under one crown, some East Lothian landowners began to have built for themselves a new style of house in which fortification played no part. This new style of house began to appear in other parts of the Lowlands but East Lothian has a particularly good collection of them. This was due in part to the fact that several of the builders were successful Edinburgh merchants or advocates who were buying their way into the landed gentry. Their ideas of a comfortable country residence were perhaps more forward-looking than those of some of their neighbours who had owned land for centuries and for whom the prestige of turrets and battlements still mattered. They were also more susceptible to architectural ideas derived from abroad or, increasingly, from England.

Despite this, the first country mansions in East Lothian scarcely resembled their counterparts south of Border. The profession of 'architect' had yet to emerge in Scotland and the masons who built them were not familiar with the new Renaissance architectural styles which were becoming fashionable on the Continent and in England. These new houses were definitely 'vernacular' in that they were built by local masons using styles and layouts which had a strong continuity with the past, incorporating many features of the earlier tower houses.

Haddington House: a fine example of a 17th-century country mansion within two minutes' walk of the centre of the burgh. The garden in the foreground has been laid out as it would have been when the house was first built.

The plans of these new houses derived directly from the towers that preceded them. The need for more space was often solved in a similar way. A common layout was a rectangular main block with a wing, forming an L-shape like many old castles. The entrance, leading to a spiral staircase, was sometimes in the angle between the wing and the main block. In other cases the projecting wing was a stair tower with a wide staircase leading to the first floor from where a turret staircase in the angle provided access to the upper floors. If more space was needed, the main block of the house could always be extended. To avoid having a house which was too long and rambling, a more elaborate plan with a wing at either end of the main block enclosing a courtyard was sometimes adopted. Many other features of the old towers can be seen in such houses. The main block and the wings were usually only one room deep and the rooms interconnected with each other rather than being reached by separate corridors. The ground floor was usually given over to the kitchens and storage space. The main living apartments were on the first floor with

121

bedrooms on the second floor and accommodation for the servants in the attics.

Two houses which stand almost opposite each other in the village of Preston are good examples of this style. Old Hamilton House (389739) was built in 1626 for Sir John Hamilton, an advocate who rose to be a Senator of the College of Justice with the title of Lord Magdalens. His wife was related by marriage to the laird of nearby Northfield House and Sir John himself to the laird who owned the adjacent tower of Preston. Sir John's house consists of a main block with projecting wings at each end whose crowstepped gables frame a courtyard bounded by a wall on the fourth side. The original entrance was in a curious semi-hexagonal tower with a pyramidal roof which is built into the angle between the main block and the west wing. The date of the house's construction, 1628, is carved in a panel above the doorway. In the angle on the opposite side of the courtyard is a well with a turret corbelled out above it. The house became split up into a number of units for the families of farm workers. As a result, little of the original interior survives but the building has been carefully restored by the National Trust for Scotland. One unusual feature of the house is that its main living rooms were on the ground floor, possibly because there was enough space for storage and other functions in the wings.

Northfield House (389739), a short distance to the west on the opposite side of the road, is also early seventeenth century in date. It was built for Joseph Majoribanks, an Edinburgh merchant. Like its neighbour it has two storeys and an attic but there is a further row of attic dormers in the steeply-pitched roof. Its plan is less complex than Sir John Hamilton's House, having a rectangular main block with a short wing forming an L-shape. Unlike Hamilton House it seems to be an older building, perhaps dating from the late sixteenth century, which has been remodelled. The original entrance, as at Hamilton House, was in a tower in the angle between the main block and the wing. The present one is comparatively recent, probably replacing an earlier one with a narrower stair. A later entrance has been made on the south side of the main block leading to a more modern staircase. Corner turrets corbelled out from the ends of the south facade echo the old baronial style of

Hamilton House, Preston. Vestiges of the old fortified style linger on in this early 17th-century laird's house.

architecture but the building is dominated by its tall chimneys and an irregular crowstepped gable which contains a doocot. The original stone-vaulted kitchen was in the main block. Its position is marked by the huge chimney stack which dominates the front of the house. A later kitchen has been built in the wing. Above the later south-facing entrance which Marjoribanks had built is the inscription 'Except the Lord build in wane builds man' with the date 1611.

The most picturesque early East Lothian mansion is the misleadingly named Penkaet Castle (425677) just outside Pencaitland. This was its original title although it is not really a castle but an undefended mansion. The name was changed to Fountainhall in 1685 when it was bought by John Lauder, another Edinburgh merchant, and his son, an advocate who became a judge with the title of Lord Fountainhall. The old house of Fountainhall is more rambling than Hamilton House or Northfield and is more composite in structure. It consists of a long main block with two wings. The long, low eastern wing is dated 1638 and the taller west wing was probably built at the end of the sixteenth century but the whole building is attractively uniform in its basic style. The west wing may originally have been a free-standing tower but has been attractively remodelled. It is three storeys high with an attic and has a curious double-pitched roof whose gables run parallel with the main block rather than at right angles to it. The east wing is entirely separate from the rest of the house internally; the upper floor is gained from the courtyard by a stone forestair. Originally this was probably a separate building which has been joined to the house by an extension of the main block. The principal entrance to the house is in the angle between the west wing and the main part of the house. On the main block are inscribed the initials J.P. and M.D. (John Pringle and his wife Margaret Dickson) with the date 1638. The north side of the house is a continuous long wall broken by a stair tower in the middle, probably marking the join between the older and newer portions of the main block. There is a doorway adjacent to the tower which is protected by a gunloop: the idea of defence had not been entirely abandoned! The house has a fine seventeenth-century walled garden on its eastern side.

When the Lauders bought the house in 1685 they had the lands around it constituted into a barony, the lowest level of jurisdiction in the old Scottish judicial system. A reminder of the legal powers which proprietors with baronies had is the pair of iron jougs attached to the south wall of the house. They were fastened round the necks of minor offenders who were left chianed up for everyone to see and ridicule! Tradition has it that the east wing of the house was used as a courtroom. It was certainly built before Fountainhall became the centre of a barony but it may well have been used by the new proprietor after 1685 to preside over his baron court.

Early seventeenth-century houses like Fountainhall are not symmetrical; that is part of their attractiveness. The idea of a balanced, uniform facade, particularly for the front of a house, came in gradually and only became firmly established in the early eighteenth century. An early example, which displays a curious mixture of old and new styles, is Pilmuir House near Bolton (486695). The house dates from 1624 and has two main storeys with an attic floor above. The ground floor is slightly

Bankton House, Prestonpans, the home of Colonel Gardiner, the dragoon commander who was killed at the battle of Prestonpans. A 19th-century monument to him stands near the house.

sunk at the front and an attractive flight of steps sweeps upwards to a central entrance at first-floor level. The windows are symmetrical around the doorway. This might seem to be a prototype Queen Anne house although the three attic dormers and the main gables have the traditional Scottish crow-steps, and the high, steeply-pitched roof has a definite seventeenth-century appearance. From the rear the traditional character of the house is evident. The main block is only one room deep and at the back there is a central wing housing a stair tower which rises a storey higher than the main part of the house. The original entrance was at the bottom of this tower, and higher up in an angle between the tower and the main block is a corbelled stair turret. The tower-house antecedents of Pilmuir are evident from this side and it appears that the new entrance to the first floor was inserted a century or so after the house was originally built.

By the time Pilmuir was being constructed, however, the new Renaissance styles of architecture were beginning to penetrate Scotland, at least for more well-to-do landowners. Winton

House (449696), just outside Pencaitland, is probably the best example of Renaissance architecture in Scotland. It was built during the 1620s to a design by William Wallace who also designed Heriot's Hospital in Edinburgh. Wallace was a master mason when the architect's task of designing houses was just beginning to separate from the mason's job of building them. The classical ornamentation of Winton House is typical of houses of its period in England but must have been novel in Scotland. The tall twisted stone chimneys can be paralleled in several English Jacobean mansions but are unique north of the Border. There seems to have been an earlier house on the site and traces of it are visible as rubble masonry. But the 1620s rebuilding is in dressed stone or ashlar, which contrasts with the more traditional rubble stonework of the houses already mentioned. In part this was a reflection of the wealth of the third Earl of Winton, who had made a lot of money from the coal mines and salt works on his lands, but it was also the start of a trend towards architecture rather than just simply building, a deliberate striving for style and effect. The plan of Winton House is simply an oblong main block with a wing at the eastern end and a stair tower projecting to the west. Inside this tower a wide turnpike stair runs to the first floor but, in traditional style, a turret stair in the angle between the tower and the main block gives access to the upper floors. As at Pilmuir the stair tower rises above the main block, ending in a balustrade with fancy corbelling. The entrance would probably originally have been at the base of the tower but a later one has been added to the north side.

Although the opportunity to admire the interiors of these seventeenth-century East Lothian mansions only arises occasionally, it is worth mentioning that the style of interior decoration also changed only slowly at this period, preserving much of its traditional character. That tapestries were still in vogue as wall decorations was shown at Fountainhall when a lath and plaster covering was stripped away to disclose one still in place. Many of the rooms here are lined with panelling of Baltic pine dating from the early eighteenth century. This had been painted in the dining room but is in its original state elsewhere. Ceilings were still ornamented by painting the exposed beams. The technique was known as tempera painting

Lennoxlove House, home of the powerful Maitland family, later Dukes of Lauderdale. Lennoxlove is a good example of how a cramped medieval tower house could be extended to provide more spacious accommodation.

and involved using a coloured glue mixture on a white background. Northfield House has the best-preserved examples in the Lothians; they were only discovered underneath later plaster in 1956. Those at Prestongrange (373737) were also discovered during alterations when a floorboard was lifted, bringing to light an old painted board-and-joist ceiling dating from 1581. The ceiling has been removed and rebuilt in the old part of Napier College, Edinburgh. Pinkie House in Musselburgh (352726) also has some fine board-and-beam ceilings painted in tempera with patterning on the beams and grotesque figures on the boards between, a common arrangement. Unfortunately, unwise restoration has darkened the best of these paintings so that they have lost their original freshness.

The First Classical Mansions

The building of the first classical mansions in Scotland, based on ideas developed by Andrea Palladio in Italy which had already been introduced to England, began in the late seventeenth century. The first exponent of the new architectural style in Scotland was also the country's first great professional architect, Sir William Bruce of Kinross, a contemporary and admirer of Sir Christopher Wren. Bruce, however, built no major new houses in East Lothian. He did a good deal of work for the Duke of Lauderdale (he was related to the Duke's formidable wife, the Countess of Dysart), and he drew up a plan for remodelling the old tower of Lethington, now Lennoxlove (515720), in 1673. The earlier part of Lennoxlove has been described in Chapter 3. The mansion is a good example of how an old medieval tower could be extended and adapted to the more gracious living conditions of the seventeenth and eighteenth centuries. The facade of the eastern part of the house, built in the early seventeenth century as a more spacious addition to the tower, has been remodelled to give it a symmetrical appearance. This may be in part the work of Bruce.

Two ruined but nevertheless interesting early examples of the new architectural influences in Scotland stand near the more traditional houses which we have described at Preston. Bankton House (395736) is famous as the home of Colonel James Gardiner, the dragoon commander at the Battle of Prestonpans (Chapter 4). It dates from the early eighteenth century. Like Pilmuir it has a sunk basement with a flight of stairs rising to the main entrance. Unlike Pilmuir, the traditional Scottish crow-steps on the gables and above the entrance have been replaced by smoothly ornamented curving ones. The symmetrical facade with a pediment over the front door and long rectangular windows owes more to southern influences than to traditional Scottish designs. A short distance away are the remains of Preston House (391739), built by the Hamiltons after a fire in their old lofty tower house in 1663 (see Chapter 3). Only a part of the front of the house survives but this shows that is was designed as a palace-style facade with two square end pavilions flanking the main block. The most

Yester House near Gifford. First planned at the end of the 17th century, the original house was rather plain and was remodelled by the Adam family.

unusual feature about this layout is that the passages linking the pavilions to the main building, instead of being built with a single curve, are S-shaped, a feature apparently unique in Scotland.

Sir William Bruce's two most important successors in the early eighteenth century were James Smith, a master mason by origin, and William Adam who had served his apprenticeship as an architect under Bruce, and whose achievements have been eclipsed by those of his famous sons. Yester House (544672), whose grounds dominate the village of Gifford, was Smith's last major building project. The original house had been a sixteenth-century tower with later additions. The second Earl of Tweeddale, later a Marquis, had discussed a replacement with Sir William Bruce and had started to remodel the policies to set it off. Construction of the house was put off for some reason and the Marquis died before a start had been made. When the second Marquis succeeded to the estate in 1697 he wanted something grander and more modern than the old tower, and work on its replacement began within a year or two. The house was not finally completed until 1728, under the fourth Marquis, a large but plain and rather dull building.

William Adam was called in almost immediately to improve it. He embellished the two main entrances by making them more prominent. But the most important contributions of William Adam and his son Robert were to the interior which they completely remodelled, making it one of the finest in Scotland. The magnificent gates to the house which frame the view down the main avenue of Gifford village were designed by Robert Adam's brother James.

The Work of the Adam Family

By the mid-eighteenth century there were still only a few new classical-style mansions in East Lothian. Gilmerton House (549778), built for the Kinloch family in the 1750s, is one of the most attractive. Inveresk Manor House (348719), built in 1748, shows how the new layout of country houses with pavilions and a central main block could co-exist with a rather coarse and plain style of decoration harking back to the seventeenth century. During the later eighteenth century, however, growing prosperity among East Lothian landowners led to an upsurge in building with older houses being extended and altered, and new ones built from scratch. Foremost among Scottish architects at this time were the Adam brothers: Robert, the most famous, and John and James. They operated throughout Britain and achieved an international reputation but have left some interesting examples of their work in East Lothian.

Their achievements at Yester House have already been mentioned. Only the shell of Archerfield House (505841), near Dirleton, now remains. The original house dates from the late seventeenth century and various architects worked on it subsequently. In 1790 Robert Adam was brought in to give the facade a facelift and reconstruct the interior, now, alas, gutted. More accessible and still complete is Lauderdale House which dominates the High Street of Dunbar. The original house was built around 1740 but was redesigned and enlarged by Robert and James Adam in the early 1790s for the Earl of Lauderdale. The High Street facade of the house is in characteristic Adam classical style. The Adams' design has suffered a little from the building's conversion to a barracks but the position at the end of the broad street is magnificent. Robert Adam was also responsible for Gosford House (453786) which he designed in 1790 for the Earl of Wemyss.

By the end of the eighteenth century the Palladian style of country house architecture was beginning to give way to other designs. The Scottish baronial style never completely disappeared between the traces of it which persisted in seventeenth- and early eighteenth-century houses like Pilmuir and its revival towards the end of the eighteenth century. It was preceded by a phase of building houses in a castle style which, despite battlements and towers, retained the symmetry and many of the design features of earlier classical houses. Seton House (418751), designed by Robert Adam in 1789, is a good example of the castle style of architecture which he developed elsewhere in Scotland during the last years of his life. Seton House was built on the site of the old palace of the Seton family which was in ruins in the later eighteenth century. The house embodies the Adam classical style in a symmetrical design with square towers flanking the entrance, and round towers at the corners.

Country Houses in the Nineteenth Century: A Mixture of Styles

During the nineteenth century the full Scottish baronial revival got under way and there are a number of houses of this type, either built from scratch or redesigned, in East Lothian. The main exponent of this style was William Burn, the most important designer of country houses in Scotland in the second quarter of the nineteenth century. Tyninghame House (621800), redesigned and extended by Burn in 1829, marks the start of the revival of this style in Scotland. Instead of the symmetry of the Adam castle style the effect here is of irregularity and a romantically jagged skyline. Burn also designed Spott House (679752) in 1830, similar in style to Tyninghame though smaller and on a superb site. Seacliff (606841) near North Berwick, which was built in 1841, was later burnt out and now forms a romantic ruin.

Although East Lothian boasts a number of Scottish baronial revival houses, the nineteenth-century pure classical style is less

common. Whittinghame House (606734), designed by Sir
Robert Smirke in 1817, is in a severe Grecian style. Jacobean
revival architecture, recalling Winton House, can be seen at
Bourhouse (669767) just outside Dunbar.

Farmhouses and Cottages Before the Nineteenth Century

What were the homes of the ordinary people of East Lothian
like in the past, and what evidence for them survives in the
landscape today? In Chapter 3 we mentioned that inside the
ramparts of several of the prehistoric hillforts in the area you
can see traces of the platforms on which circular huts were
built and sometimes their foundation too. These have survived
because their walls were built in stone and because they occupy
such high, remote locations that they have been little disturbed
since they were abandoned. Virtually none of the houses of the
ordinary farming and labouring population have survived
from the period between the abandonment of the hillforts and
the mid-eighteenth century. The reason is that they were too
squalid and flimsily built. Most of them would not have
survived for more than a few years, perhaps a generation at
most, without major repairs or rebuilding. As a result they
were easily cleared away when housing standards began to
improve in the eighteenth century.

We can get an impression of what East Lothian's farmhouses
and cottages were like before the later eighteenth century from
written accounts. An English soldier with Cromwell's army who
visited the area in the mid-seventeenth century commented on
how the farmhouses accommodated people at one end and
animals at the other. This primitive kind of dwelling, called a
'long house', had died out in most parts of England by the
sixteenth century but lasted longer in Scotland. Tenants and
cottars were expected to build their own homes with whatever
materials came to hand from the immediate vicinity. Rough
stones from the fields formed the foundations of the walls,
usually cemented with clay rather than lime mortar. Poorer
dwellings had alternate layers of stone and turf for their walls,
the turf providing a sound bedding for the rough field stones.
Clay was sometimes used as the main walling material, forming

Gosford House near Aberlady emphasises the prosperity of East Lothian landowners in the 19th century when farming reached a peak of intensiveness and efficiency.

a warm and weatherproof shell provided that it was protected from the elements. Heather or straw thatch with turf underneath covered the roof.

The walls of such houses were usually flimsy, and the weight of the roof was carried by timber arches, called crucks or 'couples', against which the walls were built. One reason for houses being poorly built was that timber for couples was in short supply and tenants usually had to depend on their landlords to provide it. Proprietors were often niggardly when it came to replacing the main timbers. A seventeenth-century survey of tenants' houses at Thornton mentions timber provided 'to John Murray's stable that fell and almost destroyed his horse' and to Adam Manderston 'for his dwelling house that fell to the ground'. Even in situations like these landlords often only supplied odd pieces of wood to shore up existing timbers. It is little wonder that none of these houses have survived!

133

Lord Belhaven, the early East Lothian improver, writing in 1699, produced a specification for an improved farmhouse with walls of stone and lime mortar rather than clay. He may have drawn his ideas from the best houses which then existed but they were probably few and far between. By the mid-eighteenth century the standard of housing had improved slightly, for the farmers at least, but most East Lothian tenants were still living in houses which we would consider mean and squalid. They were differentiated from the huts of cottars and labourers by their larger size rather than by their improved construction. A few more substantial stone houses from the late seventeenth century have survived. In Stenton, for example, there is a two-storey house dated 1692 but this was probably the home of a small owner-occupier rather than a tenant.

George Robertson, writing in 1829 and looking back to the 1760s, described the farm houses in this area on the eve of the most rapid phase of improvement. The older houses were low-built, with only a few small windows. Roofs were of straw thatch and turf and the farm dunghill was generally outside the front door. Houses of this kind were divided into two main rooms, the 'but' and the 'ben'. The first was the kitchen and servants' apartment where the entire household met at mealtimes. The ben was the farmer's private quarters where he and his family slept at night and where friends were sometimes entertained. There was usually a low attic above, for storage and as a sleeping place for the male farm servants. If this sounds primitive, it was still an improvement on earlier centuries. At least there was a proper fireplace and chimneystack in the gable instead of an open hearth in the centre of the floor and a hole in the thatch to let the smoke out, as had once been normal for farmers and was still common for their cottars. The houses of the cottars at this date were still only mean hovels with walls no more than five feet or so high made of alternate layers of field stones and turf divots. Inside the average cottar family lived in a single room only about twelve feet square.

The Revolution in Rural Housing

By the end of the eighteenth century, however, housing standards were improving rapidly as landlords and tenant profited from rising food prices caused by population growth and the Napoleonic Wars. Landlords acknowledged the need to encourage their tenant farmers by providing them with better accommodation. They allowed them enough money, usually by remission of rent at the start of a lease, for spacious new houses. Instead of being built by the farmers themselves, these improved houses were constructed by local masons with solid walls of rubble masonry, two storeys high. Instead of the old but and ben their ground floors contained a kitchen, parlour, nursery, larder and laundry with four bedrooms above and often additional space in the attics. Instead of turf and thatch they were roofed with slate. Windows were made larger and had sashes fitted. Walls were neatly plastered and lath and plaster ceilings hid the beams. Rooms were not only larger but higher. By the early nineteenth century farm houses were becoming symmetrically Georgian in appearance and offered as much comfort as a gentleman's house a couple of generations before. Although some of this first generation of improved farmsteads have survived, many were rebuilt in the mid-nineteenth century to a still higher specification.

The first concern of this new class of wealthy farmers was to improve their own homes, then to upgrade accommodation for their animals. Only latterly did they consider making the living conditions of their workers better! By the end of the eighteeenth century most farmworkers had houses with mortared stone walls, rather higher than before. In terms of their size – they usually contained only one room – and facilities they were only a slight improvement on the hovels of the earlier part of the century. From the 1840s conditions began to improve for farmworkers, though. Thatched roofs were replaced with the red pantiles which contribute so much to the East Lothian scene today. Though supposedly less warm than thatch, a tiled roof was longer-lasting and did not harbour vermin. Cottages with two apartments and sometimes a separate kitchen with attic space above a proper ceiling also became normal. The lines of farmworkers' cottages beside the larger farmsteads are a familiar sight all over the county, many of them dating from the mid-nineteenth century. They are usually single-storeyed, simple and unadorned. Being made of local materials and without any architectural affectation, they blend in superbly with the landscape. They were generally built a little way off from the farm house to emphasis the social distance between the farmer and his ploughmen.

Similar cottages were built in the villages to house craftsmen and other workers. Tyninghame and Athelstaneford have many good examples, those in the former provided by the estate to uniform designs, the ones in the latter built by individual occupiers and differing interestingly in detail. Sometimes where proprietors financed the construction of cottages they enhanced them with extra decoration like the classical-style entrances to otherwise plain houses which you can see in East Saltoun (476677). More well-to-do two-storey houses, often with slated rather than pantiled roofs, but still with the same plain features, can also be found in most East Lothian villages. In the prosperous mid-nineteenth century many new cottages were given a more consciously picturesque and pretty appearance. These cottages were often of two storeys. Good examples can be see in Dirleton where tall Tudor-type chimney stacks, deep eaves and decorated gables reflected the landlord's idiosyncratic fancies.

CHAPTER 7
Villages

East Lothian is one of the few parts of Scotland in which you can find villages of ancient origin. Over most of the country villages. For many people it is the villages above all which give the area its distinctive sense of identity with their sandstone cottages, pantiled roofs, parish kirks and mercat crosses. While many features of these villages are comparatively modern, the settlements themselves have a long and fascinating history.

Village Origins

East Lothian is one of the few parts of Scotland in which you can find villages of ancient origin. Over most of the country rural settlements are mostly scattered farms and cottages, or small hamlets. Where villages occur they are usually fairly recent creations, planned estate villages established during the eighteenth and nineteenth centuries. East Lothian, by contrast, has many villages which, although rebuilt and sometimes re-planned during the age of improvement, have much earlier origins.

These villages have a lot in common with settlements south of the Border in Northumberland. This has prompted some historians to look to the Anglian invasion and occupation of south-east Scotland between the seventh and ninth centuries A.D. as a time when such settlements may have been established. The expanding Anglian kingdom of Bernicia began to put pressure on the kingdom of Gododdin during the early seventh century and in 638 the Anglian King Oswald captued the Castle Rock of Edinburgh, their capital. The south-east corner of Scotland, particularly the coastal lowlands, was occupied for some 300 years and it was not until 1016, following the battle of Carham, that the frontier between Scotland and England was finally pushed back to the Tweed.

It was once thought that during this period the Lothians had been subjected to a full-scale colonisation from Northumbria, with an influx of peasant settlers bringing their families, farming equipment, language and customs. These colonists, it was believed, established village communities similar to the ones which they had occupied in Northumbria but very different from the scattered farms and hamlets which were normal in Scotland. According to this theory East Lothian's villages originated at this period as substantial settlements. However, recent opinion has drastically reduced the size of the invading populations in the Anglo-Saxon settlement of England. Instead of armies of tens of thousands, war bands of a few hundred are considered to have been more normal. It has been suggested that the Anglian annexation of Lothian was also more of a low-key process. Instead of a flood of immigrants who wiped out or drove off the existing population and then established new villages and fields of their own, it is now thought that there was merely a takeover at the top by a small but powerful incoming aristocracy. In such a scenario the new Anglian leaders would only have brought in a limited number of their followers. Far from displacing the existing farming population, they would have taken over their farms, settlements and estates as going concerns with a minimum of disruption and change though they would perhaps have renamed some of them in their own language.

The Anglian origins of East Lothian's villages are more evident in their names than in any visible features. Two fragment of Anglian crosses, one formerly built into the wall of the parish church of Morham (whose village has since vanished) and one in the parish church at Aberlady, are the only tangible legacy of three centuries of occupation. Nevertheless, the names of many East Lothian villages have a distinctive Northumbrian ring to them and are derived from Anglo-Saxon. The sequence in which these new names were established has been challenged but it has been suggested that among the earliest are those which ended in '-ingaham' (meaning 'settlement of the people of'). Thus we have Whittinghame (the settlement of Hvita's people) and Tyninghame (the settlement of the people living by the River Tyne). Possibly slightly later in date are names which relate to individual settlers rather than groups, with '-ington' ('the settlement of') preceded by a personal name. Haddington may

The village of Stenton preserves a layout which may go back to medieval times.

be one of these. Other Anglian village names incorporate '-ham' (a settlement): Morham, Oldhamstocks; '-botl' ('a dwelling'): Bolton; and '-wic' ('a farm'): North Berwick (barley farm).

Not all Anglian place names are attached to villages; some relate to smaller places. Nevertheless two features of these names are striking when you look at them on a map: their distribution and the importance of the places which bear them. They are all in the fertile lowlands. There are none in the Lammermuirs which may have been left to the native inhabitants. A high proportion of Anglian names are attached to places which in medieval times were substantial villages and the centres of their respective parishes. Such places are also likely to have been important in earlier times and it looks as if the Anglians took over and renamed the centres of existing estates. This does not work invariably of course; some places which were important in medieval times retained British names, like Aberlady, Dunbar and Tranent. The overall impression is that Anglian place names are not very thick on the ground and that their settlement was a correspondingly light one with the resident population being left largely undisturbed.

So what of the 'Anglian' villages of East Lothian? It is impossible to show convincingly that they originated at this period, but the idea cannot be totally disproved either. The earliest documentary records show that they were village-sized in medieval times, though not necessarily with the same layout as today. But there is a gap of some 600 years between the Anglian colonisation of the area and the first documents relating to them, a gap during which many changes could have occurred in the ways in which such places were laid out and in their importance. Without excavation it is unlikely that we will ever be certain whether East Lothian's villages owe their origins to the Anglian conquerers or not.

The plans of East Lothian villages, particularly the greens around which the buildings of some of them are ranged, also suggest links with Northern England where village greens are common. For some English villages the layout around a green has been shown to go back to medieval times, though village greens are unlikely to have originated during the Anglo-Saxon period as was once thought. Do the plans of East Lothian villages have a similar antiquity? For Dirleton with its large green it is possible to use estate rentals and other documents to show that the layout of the village during the late sixteenth and early seventeenth centuries was similar to that of the present day. This at least proves that the green was not created as part of some later estate-planning scheme, and if it existed in the sixteenth century it might well go back to medieval times; but the documentary record peters out and does not allow this suggestion to be proved. Documentary evidence also shows that

The mercat cross in Preston village, with its ornate base, is one of the most attractive in Scotland. It dates from the early 17th century.

the single-street village of Stenton had the same basic layout in the mid-sixteenth century.

Burghs of Barony and Market Centres

During medieval times and indeed much later East Lothian's villages were primarily agricultural settlements, their inhabitants being mostly farmers, cottagers and labourers with only a few craftsmen serving local needs. But the villages were also focal points; people gathered in them every Sunday to attend the kirk, people visited the landowner's castle or mansion nearby and attended his baron court, people travelling between the towns also stopped in them overnight. Even in a primitive rural society no family could produce all the items which it needed; trade, even if only on a small scale, was essential and the villages were the obvious central locations for buying and selling.

The villages were probably market centres from ancient times but during the seventeenth century, with the development of a more commercial economy and slowly increasing prosperity among the rural population, there was a growth of trading throughout the countryside. This was highlighted by the granting of market rights to many rural settlements. By the early eighteenth century most of East Lothian's villages had acqured the right to hold markets and fairs. The earliest grants carried with them the title 'burgh of barony' and their proprietors had the right, if they chose to exercise it, of planning a fully-fledged town and endowing it with burgesses, a council and a burgh court. The only baronial burghs which grew in this way were the coal- and salt-producing centres of Tranent, which received its charter in 1541/2, Prestonpans (1552) and Cockenzie (1591) along with Musselburgh, a much earlier foundation (between 1315 and 1328).

Where villages were purely agricultural without any significant industry it is doubtful if there was ever a serious intention by their proprietors to try and turn them into towns. Most of them merely held weekly markets and one or two annual fairs which served the farms within the parish. Seton (1321), Dunglass (1489), Pencaitland (1505), Tyninghame (1591), Drem (1616), Innerwick (1630) and Dirleton (1631) were all elevated to the status of burghs but remained villages in size and functions. During the later seventeenth century a number of other villages were granted market rights without the pretentious title of burgh. These included Ormiston and Stenton (1669), Oldhamstocks and East Linton (1672), Penston (1690) and Athelstaneford (1707).

Whether designated a burgh of barony or merely a licensed market centre, the symbol of a village's right to carry on trade was the mercat cross. The mercat cross has not survived in every village: in Aberlady the head of the cross has been truncated and only 2m of the shaft remains on its base. The finest cross in East Lothian and one of the best in Scotland is at Preston (389739). It stands in the main street on a stone drum 3.7m high which is divided into niches, six of which contain seats and two of which have doorways. One door leads into a small room, the others to steps giving access to a platform with a corbelled parapet from which proclamations were read. The shaft rises from this rotunda and is topped by a unicorn holding up a tablet bearing the design of a lion rampant. It is thought that the cross at Preston was built shortly after 1617

The mercat cross at Ormiston probably incorporates a cross belonging to an earlier chapel which stood nearby.

when the village obtained the right to hold a market and fair. Many of these 'crosses', like the one at Preston, were not actually topped by a cross; the one at Gifford (535682) has a stone ball on top, while the 'cross' at Wester Pencaitland (442689) is actually a sundial! A genuine cross stands in the main street of Ormiston (416694). Ormiston obtained its market rights in 1669 but the cross is much earlier, probably dating from the fifteenth century. It is one of the few pre-Reformation crosses surviving in Scotland. It is possible that it originally stood outside a chapel which is known to have been sited near here.

Lost Villages

The fact that so many of East Lothian's villages have ancient names and have survived the vicissitudes of political, economic and social changes throughout the centuries testifies to their durability, but the county also has its share of lost villages whose sites are now under the plough and whose very existance has been forgotton by most people. The most striking example, marked as a deserted village on large-scale Ordnance Survey

maps (though not on the 1:50,000 Landranger map), is
Morham (557722). If you visit the site today you can still find
the parish kirk (557727). It is hard to find, down an ever-
narrowing lane hidden by trees in a sheltered hollow. It is an
attractive little church dating from 1724 but there are older
tombstones in the churchyard to show that there must have
been an earlier church here. The fragment of an Anglian cross
shaft formerly built into the wall of the present church
indicates that the site is very ancient. The map also marks the
site of Morham Castle (557723) while the Mill Bridge across the
Morham Burn indicates the former existence of the village
grain mill.

When did Morham disappear and why did it vanish? The
minister who wrote the parish report for the Old Statistical
Account during the 1790s stated that no village existed at that
time. However, there were still a few houses near the site of the
castle and some cottages a quarter of a mile away called West
Gate End, a name which has since disappeared from the map.
The small size of the parish and its church, which was even
smaller than the manse, suggests that the village cannot have
been large when the new kirk was built in 1724. It seems likely,
then, that Morham declined gradually over a long period
instead of being abandoned at a particular date. The couple of
clusters of cottages in the late eighteenth century were
probably the last vestiges of the former settlement whose extent
and layout are still uncertain.

While Morham may have declined gradually, other villages
were deserted more swiftly. The old settlement of Bothans
near Yester House (544672) is an example. It was the main
settlement of the parish of that name until the later
seventeenth century when the Marquis of Tweeddale cleared it
and re-established the inhabitants in the new village of Gifford
a kilometre to the north-west. The name of the parish was
changed from Bothans to Yester with the disppearance of the
old village. It is probable that something similar happened at
Bara, the parish and church of which was merged with that of
Garvald in 1702. Today the site of Bara church (558706) lies in
a corner of a field on a hillslope looking northwards towards
Morham but the church itself has vanished, as have any surface
traces of the settlement which must surely have adjoined it. At

The small parish church at Morham, hidden down a narrow lane, survives although the village which it once served has vanished.

Tyninghame the old village was also moved further away from the estate mansion and rebuilt by the proprietor. The former village of Winton was also moved but was never rebuilt. Pitcox (642753) near Biel House may be an example of a shrunken village, for today it has only half a dozen cottages and a single farmstead set around a small triangular green, but originally it was a substantial village with a church of its own and gave its name to the parish which is now known by that of another village, Spott. The parish chruch was moved at the Reformation and the village declined.

Estate Villages

During the later eighteenth and early nineteenth centuries over 300 new villages were laid out on estates all over Scotland.
Their aim was in some cases to provide new centres for marketing agricultural produce. Often the intention was to establish rural industry, especially textiles, which could provide employment for estate inhabitants who were being forced out of farming with the changes which were taking place in agriculture. Some of these new settlements remained small

while others were more successful until the concentration of textile manufacturers in factories in the towns.

The Scottish planned village movement began in East Lothian during the 1730s. At this time John Cockburn of Ormiston, who had already been improving his estates for some years (Chapter 5), decided to rebuilt Ormiston as a model community along the lines of an English village. He employed an English land surveyor, Lewis Gordon, to lay out the new settlement and its surrounding fields. The result can still be seen in the modern village: a single tree-lined main street, wide enough for markets to be held, and closed off at each end by right-angled bends in the road. Some of the new houses in Ormiston were built at Cockburn's expense, others by people to whom he granted plots of land. Where the houses were built by their occupiers Cockburn provided the building materials and stipulated that the dwellings should be of high quality: two storeys, of mortared stone, and with slate roofs. This was a time when single-storeyed thatched cottages were normal in East Lothian villages. Ormiston had a variety of industries providing employment apart from the spinning and weaving of linen. There was a brewery and a distillery as well as an extensive bleachfield, one of the first in Scotland. Although the layout of the centre of Ormiston has not changed since Cockburn's time, many of the houses have been replaced. However, if you walk down the tree-lined avenue you can still find some which seems to be early enough to have been built during Cockburn's lifetime.

Although East Lothian already had many villages, and did not require any additional planned settlements, existing villages were nevertheless improved by their proprietors. It is this 'estate village' character rather than their more ancient origins which comes out strongly when you visit them. The most completely re-modelled estate village is Tyninghame, whose buildings were mainly constructed during the first three decades of the nineteenth century. Tyninghame is a good example of an estate village whose development was rigidly controlled by the proprietor. The harled factor's house dates from about 1800 and the lodge and gateway to Tyninghame House beside it are slightly later. On the other side of the road the estate sawmill, which was powered by a water wheel, is still

These estate cottages in East Saltoun village are a good example of how landowners ornamented and embellished the houses of their labourers to make showpieces of their villages.

in use as a private house and was built in 1828. It was designed by Thomas Hannan, as were most of the cottages as well as the school and the village hall.

Athelstaneford was also given a facelift during the main period of agricultural improvement. Landlord control was more relaxed here than at Tyninghame and much of the work was done by individual developers, not the estate. Sir David Hamilton of Kinloch leased off plots in the village at moderate rents to people who would build good-quality houses to replace what the local minister described as 'small, dirty, dark hovels'. Each householder had a back garden and a big enough share in a hundred-acre plot of land to grow potatoes, raise some oats, or keep a cow. This was common in planned villages, many of whose tradesmen inhabitants were also smallholders. The result of each householder building his own property under a set of general guidelines is evident today. The cottages are mostly single-storey with rubble walls and pantiled roofs but they exhibit interesting differences in detail, a feature which contrasts attractively with more formal creations like Tyninghame. A notable characteristic of Athelstaneford, and other East Lothian villages, is the absence of front gardens, something which William Cobbett, accustomed to the gardens of English cottagers, found unusual. The reason was that most landowners prohibited them; they feared that, particularly where the owners were smallholders, they would follow the old farming custom of having the dunghill at their front door, a feature which was not in keeping with their plans for the appearance of their new model communities!

Although Ormiston is often considered the first planned village of the era of improvement, Gifford is an interesting example of a newly-created village from a slightly earlier date. During the late seventeenth century the Marquis of Tweeddale was laying out extensive plantations and parks around the old Yester House in preparation for rebuilding the mansion. As we have mentioned, the settlement of Bothans with its parish church was inconveniently close to the 'big house', so the Marquis had it moved to a site at the gates of his new park. In 1710 he had a new parish church built for the transposed community on a site which dominates the short main street with the mercat cross at the opposite end. Originally the new village was laid out as lines of smallholdings with a house on each plot along the roadside. During the nineteenth century, however, pressure on the available space caused some of these plots to be subdivided and new houses inserted in the gaps between the older ones. This alteration of older and newer houses is a feature to look out for today. The settlement was designed by its proprietor and is still dominated by Yester House and its grounds with a wide avenue of lime trees leading from the mercat cross towards the mansion. The grassy area between the Avenue and the High Street was once a bleaching green. There are no houses from the earliest phase of the new settlement though near the cross are two houses which appear to date from the early eighteenth century.

Other East Lothian villages were not toally rebuilt but had a good deal of money invested in them by their proprietors. Aberlady has rows of estate cottages in a Gothic style dating from the 1830s while in Dirleton there is an interesting contrast between the plain, solid cottages from the early nineteenth century and the more ornate picturesque-style ones of a generation later.

East Linton. The inscription on the fountain reads: 'Presented to the Burgh of East Linton by John Drysdale Esq., Buenos Ayres. 1882'.

Villages in Modern Times

Most East Lothian villages reached their peak of population during the later eighteenth and early nineteenth centuries. At this time the rapid commercialisation of agriculture and the general rise in standards of living provided plenty of work for village craftsmen like blacksmiths, wrights, masons, and shoemakers. There was also a good deal of handloom weaving before textile manufacturing became concentrated in the towns, while larger villages like East Linton were important milling centres had surprisingly large populations considering that they were only agricultural service centres. Looking down the main street of Ormiston, it is difficult to imagine it having a population of nearly 600 at the end of the eighteenth century but many people were employed in weaving, spinning linen yarn or bleaching. By the 1830s the population of Ormiston had fallen markedly due to the drift to the towns.

Thereafter for much of the nineteenth and early twentieth centuries the story in many villages was one of gradual depopulation and decline, particularly in the more remote

149

settlements, checked only temporarily by improvements in mobility brought by the railways, the bicycle, and motor bus services. During the twentieth century many of the older cottages, which were often damp without inside toilets, were demolished and almost every village acquired some council houses on its outskirts as a replacement. Some are brick-built, contrasting with the warm red or pink sandstone rubble masonry of the old cottages, but others are built in traditional style with local stone and pantiled roofs. These council houses, varying from groups of three or four in villages like Stenton to large estates in Pencaitland, were an attempt to provide better-quality housing for rural workers. More recently, however, the trend has been towards improving the older cottages, and the designation of many village centres as conservation areas has helped to preserve their traditional character.

Some villages have managed to remain small and purely rural, particularly those along the edge of the Lammermuirs: East Saltoun, Garvald, Gifford, Innerwick, Oldhamstocks, Spott, and Stenton. Most of these are off the beaten track. Some, like Oldhamstocks, or Garvald, nestling in a sheltered valley, are positively hidden so that you have to seek them out. By contrast, many villages on the coastal plain have been affected by non-rural developments. At Preston this happened at an early date as the focus of the settlement shifted from the old village centre towards the coal-mining and salt-producing burgh of Prestonpans. Preston still retains something of its village character with its fine mercat cross, the fifteenth-century tower house, and the mansions of Hamilton House, Preston House and Northfield House. The curious thing is that there is so little ordinary housing left, but the group of buildings is nevertheless a fine one, and rather unexpected on the edge of an industrial centre.

John Cockburn's planned community of Ormiston changed with the opening of the Ormiston Coal Company in 1903, becoming a mining settlement. Similar changes happened at Wester Pencaitland. Penston was a mining village in the seventeenth century when colliers were still officially serfs who could be bought and sold with the pits. In 1690 a market and two annual fairs were authorised there because of the eighty colliers and their families (suggesting a total population of perhaps 300-400) were so restricted in their mobility that they were unable to attend markets at Tranent only 4km away. The development of the coalfield in the nineteenth century led to the creation of totally new mining villages like Elphinstone, whose population rose to over 800, and Macmerry. The closure of the pits in this area since the Second World War has led to a decline of population in most of these centres.

With the coming of the railway (Chapter 10) Gullane developed as a resort and golfing centre. Longniddry, which had declined to a couple of rows of cottages, is now a commuter settlement for Edinburgh with large new housing estates. During the nineteenth century East Linton, with the advantage of its siting beside the main road through the county, and later the railway, developed as an important local market centre. It was here that migrant harvest workers, many from the Highlands and Ireland, were hired each week. These incomers were sometimes so boisterous that parties of dragoons had to be sent from Edinburgh to maintain order. East Linton's nineteenth-century prosperity is still evident in its market hall and its solid two-storey houses which contrast with the single-storey cottages of other villages.

A quiet corner in Aberlady, showing the Wagon Inn.

CHAPTER 8
Towns

Although East Lothian is primarily a rural county, towns have been important to its inhabitants from medieval times. One could make a case for counting the settlement on Traprain Law, occupied from the late Bronze Age into the post-Roman period (Chapter 3), as East Lothian's first town. Traprain was abandoned during the Dark Ages, though, and urban life did not begin to develop again until the twelfth century. It was then that David I and his successors developed the idea of establishing burghs, or planned trading communities, on the model which the Normans had imported into England.

By the end of the thirteenth century Scottish monarchs, along with lay and ecclesiastical landowners, had laid out a network of these new settlements throughout the Lowlands. Haddington was the first of these foundations in East Lothian, and over the centuries others like Dunbar, North Berwick and Musselburgh were established. They functioned as centres for crafts and industries, places where crops and livestock could be marketed, and through which items not produced locally could be imported. In the sixteenth and seventeenth centuries, a new class of upstart burgh began to appear in Scotland. These burghs of barony, holding their charters from local landowners rather than the crown, were in many cases linked to new industrial developments. The rise of the coal and salt industries in East Lothian led to the development of Prestonpans, Cockenzie and later Tranent.

The old-established centres proved remarkably resilient in the face of this competition. Haddington, Dunbar and Musselburgh each developed in their own distinctive ways from the seventeenth century onwards. The history of East Lothian is reflected in its townscapes as much as in its countryside, for town and country have always been intimately linked. In this chapter we look at some of East Lothian's towns as they appear today and try to discover something of their past. In other chapters we have pursued particular themes across the county rather than covering the area in a place-by-place gazetteer.

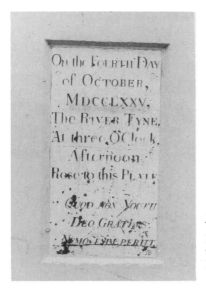

On the FOURTH Day
of OCTOBER,
MDCCLXXV,
The River TYNE,
At three O'Clock,
Afternoon
Rose to this PLATE

Quod non Jacru
Deo Gratias
Memor Lyne Peritt

This plaque near the centre of Haddington indicates the burgh's vulnerability to flooding by the River Tyne; on this occasion in 1775.

However, given that the towns we are going to consider have their own distinctive personalities, we have treated each one separately to avoid overlap and confusion.

Haddington

Haddington is the oldest of East Lothian's burghs and for centuries has been the county town, the focus for much of the economic and social life of the area. Because of its limited growth since the eighteenth century, the town has preserved much of its traditional atmosphere. Sensitive restoration and landscaping in recent years have made it one of the most attractive of Scotland's older burghs. Haddington was founded sometime between 1124 and 1153 by David I, and apart from a brief period later in the twelfth century, when it was granted to Countess Ada, the mother of Malcolm IV, it has always been a royal burgh. Supposedly the town originally grew up around the palace in which Alexander II was born in 1198. The site of this palace is thought to have been where the County Buildings in Court Street now stand, but no remains of this early royal centre have survived.

Throughout its history Haddington suffered from two major disadvantages in terms of its location. The first was lack of access to the sea. At an early date the burgh was granted Aberlady as a dependent port. Aberlady was not the best of natural harbours, but in the days when most seagoing vessels were small this was not a major drawback. Haddington's other disadvantage was its vulnerable position on the direct line of march of invading English armies. As one poet put it:

Next unto Berwick, Haddington faced all,
The greatest dangers and was Scotland's wall.

Haddington was burnt by the English four times during the thirteenth and fourteenth centuries, and again in the 1540s.

Haddington had been one of Scotland's foremost burghs in late medieval times. However, the siege of 1548-49 (Chapter 4) left the town in ruins. Although the burgesses rebuilt their homes and resumed their trades and crafts, the scars caused by the siege were slow to disappear and the town does not seem to have regained its former prosperity. Travellers found Haddington rather decayed. Daniel Defoe, visiting it early in the eighteenth century, described it as 'an old, half ruined . . . town which shows the marks of decayed beauty, for it was formerly a large, handsome and well built town'. He also noted, however, that 'Haddington is still a good town, has some handsome streets and well built, and they have a good stone bridge over the Tyne'. The bastions thrown up by the English garrison in 1548-9 were still visible along with the town's own stone wall. The siege and the Reformation had dealt harshly with the burgh kirk which was still half ruined in Defoe's day. He was impressed with the Newmills cloth manufactory (Chapter 9), the first industry which he had come across since he entered Scotland, but he shrewdly commented: 'they really make very good cloth . . . but I cannot say that they make it cheap . . . as the English'.

By the end of the eighteenth century Haddington was prosperous once more. If the town did not thrive as a centre of industry, then this was compensated by the effects of agricultural improvement in the surrounding area (Chapter 5). Haddington became the most important grain market in

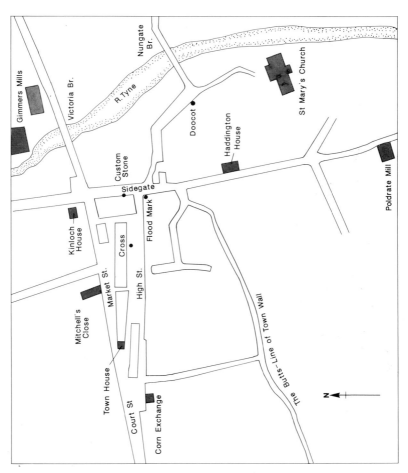

Map 11. Plan of Haddington.

Scotland, serving the most advanced and go-ahead farming area in the country. When William Cobbett visited Haddington in 1833 he was struck by the 'innumberable carts carrying corn towards that town' which he met on the roads. The burgh itself was 'a large, good and solid town . . . an immense mart for corn'. Its situation close to the main post road to England gave it a flourishing coaching trade. The coming of the railway in the 1840s brought this period of prosperity to an end. The main line from Edinburgh to Berwick by-passed the town which was only linked by a branch line – even then with a station well away from the town centre. Grain which had formerly come to Haddington by cart now went to Edinburgh or Glasgow by rail. Haddington became once more a sleepy country town, a quiet backwater. In recent years, however, this image has changed. Since the Second World War a lot of effort has been directed into the sensitive restoration and conservation of many of the town's historic buildings so that it is now one of the most attractive of Scotland's older burghs. With the great increase in car ownership in the post-war period Haddington has been brought within the commuting orbit of Edinburgh, as is shown by the new housing estates which have developed on its outskirts.

The town is situated on a river terrace at the foot of the Garleton Hills with the River Tyne flowing around it to the south and east. The Tyne has been important in Haddington's history as the source of power for a string of mills grinding grain, fulling cloth and doing other kinds of work (Chapter 9). The river may look gentle and innocuous but it is capable of violent spates on occasion. The sixteenth-century Nungate Bridge was the only stone bridge across the river at Haddington until the nineteenth century, probably due to the river's tendency to occasional but severe floods. One of these occurred in 1421 when most of the town was damaged. An even more serious flood happened in 1775, supposedly due to a waterspout at Gifford. The height to which the river rose – seventeen feet above its normal level – is marked by a plaque on the corner of Sidegate and the High Street. Worst of all was the flood of 12th–13th August 1948 in which the Tyne rose above all previously recorded levels to form a raging tide some 800 yards across. Many people in the lower part of the town

Mitchell's Close, Haddington. A good example of how the tails of the burgage plots behind the buildings fronting on the main streets have been filled in by workshops and small businesses.

were made homeless and a layer of mud a foot deep was deposited in the streets by the retreating water.

The layout of the centre of Haddington has all the classic elements of a medieval Scottish burgh. The main street was originally a huge triangular market place where now Court Street, Market Street, High Street and the buildings between stand. Its base was terminated by the line of Hardgate and Sidegate running at right angles, and it tapered away westwards into the road leading out towards the burgh's common pastures at Gladmuir. The centre of the burgh is spacious enough today even with all the infilling that has taken place, so the original market area must have been really impressive. During the fifteenth and sixteenth centuries a gradual infilling of the market place occurred with temporary stalls being replaced by more permanent buildings. This early infilling was in turn replaced from the seventeenth century by even more substantial buildings producing the island of shops and houses which fill up the old market place today.

Haddington's role as a market centre is still commemorated in the mercat cross in the High Street, adorned with the famous Haddington goat, the traditional symbol of the town.

The cross dates from the later nineteenth century, replacing a series of older ones. At the junction of High Street and Hardgate is the medieval Custom Stone at which market tolls were paid. Haddington was also an adminstrative centre, the seat of the burgh and sheriff courts. At the top of the west arch on the Nungate Bridge you can see an iron hook which was used for hanging criminals convicted by the courts. Its use is well attested in the burgh records; for instance, at the funeral of the notorious Duke of Lauderdale in the seventeenth century money was scattered to the poor, and in a fight over the spoils one beggar stabbed another with a knife and killed him. The beggar was promptly tried and hanged from the bridge.

On either side of the main street lines of building plots ran back at right angles forming a herringbone pattern. These were known as 'burgages' and originally everyone who was admitted as a burgess of the town would have occupied one. To the south these plots terminated against an area of open ground known as the Butts, where archery was formerly practised. To the north, between Newton Port and Hardgate, you can still see a short section of the wall (515742) which ran along the bottom of the plots and provided the town with a rudimentary defence, or at least a means of regulating the admittance of undesirables. This wall was originally known as the King's Wall and dates from the fifteenth century. To the south of the town centre the line of the former wall is clearly marked by a lane called the Butts. The walls were pierced with gates or 'ports': there was formerly a South Port at the foot of Sidegate which was demolished in 1766. At the West Port, on the road to Edinburgh, a toll house and gate were built to collect customs on produce being brought into the town on market days. The toll house stood in what is now called the West End where a statue of Robert Ferguson of Raith is now sited. There was also a North-East Port at the end of Hardgate.

Originally only the frontages facing on to the market place were built up and the rear of the burgage plots were open with gardens and smallholdings. As time went on and pressure for accommodation grew, additional houses and workshops were constructed and the plots began to be built over. These new properties required access from the main street so that alleys or

Kinloch House, Haddington, has curving gables reflecting Dutch architectural influences. It was originally built as the town house for a local landowning family.

'closes' were built between and below the buildings fronting on the market place. If you explore them you will see that many of these closes are named after local families who owned the street frontages from which they led off. Mitchell's Close, near the junction of Market Street and Newton Port, gives a good idea of how the burgages developed. Behind the main properties which face on to the market place you can see on either side of the close lower ranges of buildings which were formerly workshops – one with an outside stone staircase – and which have been attractively restored. Because the centre of Haddington never became heavily built up this pattern of plot boundaries and the buildings between them is more readily visible than in most other Scottish towns.

In medieval times most of the houses in the burgh were of timber-frame construction with thatched roofs. During the sixteenth and seventeenth centuries, with growing prosperity among the town's merchants and craftsmen, these houses were rebuilt in stone, their gables generally facing on to the main street. Many of them once had outside stone forestairs leading to the first floor but these were mostly removed during the later eighteenth century. Some seventeenth-century houses have survived with relatively little alteration but many were re-fronted during the eighteenth and early nineteenth centuries. This was the period when Haddington, as the main market centre in the most advanced farming region of Scotland, reached its peak of prosperity. A walk through the centre of the burgh today gives you the impression of a largely Georgian town, with some Victorian additions and modern shop fronts. Although some fine houses were built at this time, a good deal of older work underlies this Georgian facade. You can see this clearly in Mitchell's Close where the backs of the main properties, with their crow-stepped gables, are much older in style than their Market Street facades. The smart appearance of the main street is a tribute to the conservation and restoration work which the town's authorities have set in motion during recent years.

At the corner of Market Street and Hardgate is the attractive early eighteenth-century Kinloch House, built as a town house for the Kinloch family whose estate at Gilmerton was only a short distance away. This emphasises Haddington's importance as a social centre for local landowners. The house is an early example of a symmetrical facade, dominated in this case by a central chimney stack, with Dutch-style curved gables.

Haddington's former importance as a stagecoach centre is shown by the number of old coaching inns. The George, 91 High Street, was always the main inn of the burgh, which was the first stage for changing horses on the road from Edinburgh. No 43-45 High Street was formerly the Bluebell Inn where the Edinburgh to Newcastle coach stopped, and no 73, now the Commercial Hotel, was formerly the Britannia. The Victoria Inn stands on the island which blocks the eastern end of Court Street. The Castle Hotel, dating from the eighteenth century, stands at the east end of the High Street.

The focal building in the centre of the burgh is the Town House. It was designed by William Adam in 1752 but it has been altered since then with a courtroom added to the west in 1788 and a steeple by Gillespie Graham in 1831. The County Buildings in Tudor Revival style by William Burn, who designed many country houses in the surrounding area

The frontages of these houses in the centre of Haddington are Georgian but a good deal of the stonework at the sides and rear is older.

(Chapter 6), date from 1832. Next to them is the classical-style Corn Exchange of 1853. Previously all the grain which came into the burgh on market day was sold in the main streets, causing tremendous congestion, and the Corn Exchange was designed to relieve this pressure. The cattle market was shifted from the town centre out to the station at around the same time.

Haddington's imposing burgh kirk, St. Mary's, almost a cathedral in scale, stands well away from the town centre in a magnificent setting by the river. By the time it was built, in the mid-fifteenth century, there may already have been a shortage of space around the market place. The church is described in Chapter 2. In Church Street, between St. Mary's and the High Street, the Holy Trinity Episcopal church stands on the site of the ancient friary church which was known as 'The Lamp of Lothian', possibly due to the magificence of its stained glass, but which was destroyed by the English in the fourteenth century (Chapter 2).

On the east of Sidegate is Haddington House, an early seventeenth-century laird's house on an L-plan (see Chapter 6) with a tower stair and crow-stepped gables. The original entrance was at the base of the tower stair at the rear but a later one has been made from Sidegate. The building has been attractively restored in recent years and is now the headquarters of the Lamp of Lothian Collegiate Trust. Behind it and to one side the area of St. Mary's Pleasance has been turned into a traditional seventeenth-century Scottish garden. This contains a variety of herbs with labels showing some of the traditional uses to which they were put. Some of these are bizarre in the extreme and there is a notice warning curious visitors not to try them out for themselves!

Along the river, both upstream and downstream of St. Mary's, are a series of mills reflecting Haddington's industrial past. These are described in detail in Chapter 9.

Dunbar

Like Haddington, Dunbar is an ancient royal burgh. It originated more modestly in the thirteenth century as a burgh of barony belonging to the Earls of March, growing up in the shadow of their formidable castle (Chapter 3), and was forfeited to the crown along with the rest of the earldom in the fifteenth century. It became a royal burgh in 1445 and ever since has served as Haddington's counterpart, the main market centre for the eastern part of the county. Dunbar had the distinct advantage over its rival of being sited on the coast. However, as we describe in Chapter 10, the original harbour was small and difficult of access; despite subsequent construction schemes it still seems tiny by modern standards. standards.

Dunbar was burnt to the ground by the English during the invasions of 1544 and 1548 and suffered the added misfortune of being occupied by Cromwell's army in 1650 prior to the Battle of Dunbar (Chapter 4). Although Cromwell did not damage the burgh, he did commandeer most of its shipping and, like Haddington, it took a long time to get back on its feet. When John Ray visited it in 1662 he described it as 'quite ruined and fallen down', and it seemed to have remained in this state for much of the later seventeenth century. By the

Haddington's former position as the premier grain market in Scotland is reflected by these old granaries.

early eighteenth century the success of the herring fishery was bringing some prosperity back to the town. When the migratory herring shoals reached this part of the coast in August or September there were sometimes 300 fishing vessels operating offshore from the town. Later in the eighteenth century Dunbar was a notable whaling centre, sending its boats to the cold waters of the Davis Strait. Defoe described it as 'a handsome, well-built town'. Like Haddington, Dunbar's fortunes picked up later in the century when the modernisation of agriculture in the county turned it into a major market centre for grain. Grain formed the main item of export and Cobbett, approaching the town from the south in 1833, found 'the road . . . covered with carts . . . all loaded with sacks of corn. For several miles it appeared to be a regular convoy of carts . . . and all going to Dunbar'. He thought Dunbar an attractive town: 'the main stret is so wide', he wrote, 'as to be worthy of being called an oblong square'.

The vulnerability of this coast to enemy attack was demonstrated in 1779 when John Paul Jones, the American Revolutionary sea commander, appeared off Dunbar with a squadron of five ships and in 1781 when another adventurer,

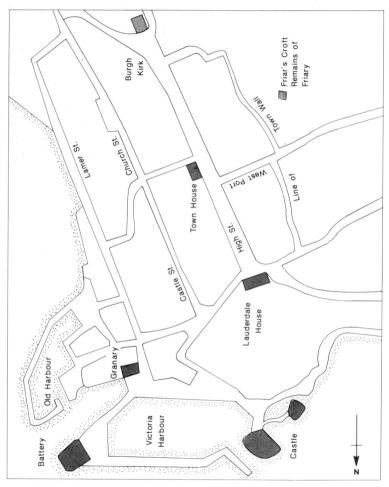

Map 12. Plan of Dunbar.

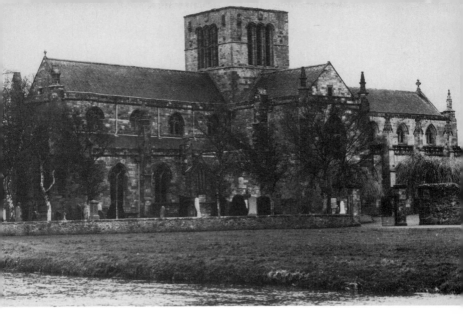

St Mary's church, Haddington, one of the finest burgh kirks in Scotland and almost a cathedral in scale, has a magnificent setting beside the peaceful waters of the River Tyne.

Captain Fall, tried to carry off a vessel from the mouth of the harbour. The defence of the town was improved by installing a battery of sixteen cannon to protect the harbour. When Napoleon was threatening to invade Britain there was a fear that Belhaven Bay might be a suitable landing place. A barracks, designed to accommodate 1,200 infantry, was built near the harbour with another at Belhaven for 300 cavalry. The invasion never materialised but Dunbar remained a garrison centre until recent times.

In 1844 the town sold most of its common pastures in the Lammermuirs to finance construction of the Victoria Harbour. This encouraged the local fishing industry and allowed the town's trade to expand. During the nineteenth century an important seaborne trade in potatoes developed with London. The coming of the railway helped the town to develop into a holiday resort, capitalising on the fact that Dunbar is one of the driest and sunniest places in Scotland. The town was only a short journey by train from Edinburgh and people could visit it for day trips as well as stay for longer periods. The large villas on the western outskirts of the town testify to the prosperity of Dunbar in the nineteenth century.

Today the harbour is a quiet place with only a few fishing vessels; the herring fleets, the whalers, the grain trade and the cargoes of potatoes are long gone. The harbour itself, with the ruins of the castle and the old warehouse and maltings which surround it (Chapter 10), is a peaceful and picturesque scene. The original nucleus of the town may have been here, close under the gates of the castle (Chapter 3). There are indications that the present High Street may have been laid out at a later date, probably early in the seventeenth century. The High Street which so impressed Cobbett is still broad and wide. It is dominated at its northern end by Lauderdale House, an impressive country mansion which looks slightly out of place in an urban setting. In the early eighteenth century there was a mansion here owned by the Fall family, wealthy Dunbar merchants. They were obliged to sell it in 1788 and Robert Adam had it altered and enlarged for the Duke of Lauderdale. In the middle of the nineteenth century it was converted to a military headquarters with a barracks and barrack square adjacent.

At the south end of the High Street is the Abbey Church built in 1850 and formerly belonging to the Free Church rather than the Church of Scotland. As at Haddington, Dunbar's burgh kirk (Chapter 2) is set away from the main street. Here, though, the medieval collegiate kirk founded by the Earls of Dunbar in 1342 has been replaced by an early nineteenth-century building. Its Gothic battlements and towers make it a distinctive building and a prominent landmark when seen from the sea. Sadly, the church was gutted by fire in January 1987, although it is hoped to restore it and to save the fine marble memorial to the Earl of Dunbar which was damaged by the heat. Halfway along the east side of the High Street stands the old tolbooth. Built around 1620, it combined the functions of council chamber, toll house and prison. The ground floor of the three-storey block is vaulted. Market tolls were collected from offices on the ground floor and the council chamber was located above. The gables are crow-stepped in a style which recalls Dutch architecture; Dunbar exported grain to the Low Countries during the seventeenth century. The front of the building is dominated by a five-sided stair tower rising to a steeple. Old photographs show two lean-to shops

Haddington's town house and other buildings filling in what was once a huge open market place.

built on either side of the steeple, and their removal has improved the appearance of the tolbooth. In front of the tolbooth stands the mercat cross of the burgh. The character of the High Street is mainly eighteenth and nineteenth century, but if you walk down some of the closes to the rear of the building plots, you can see some older work behind.

Dunbar was once a walled town like Haddington. In the late seventeenth century a visitor described the burgh as 'fenced in by a stone wall of great strength' though 'much impaired and gone to decay'. Little of this wall has survived. The name 'West Port' given to a street which enters the High Street almost opposite the tolbooth reminds us of the location of one of the former gates to the town. There was also a south port at the bottom of the High Street and another gateway on the east side of the High Street. This may originally have marked the western limits of the burgh before the new High Street was laid out. These ports were standing in 1768 but were demolished not long after. Down Bamburgh's Close, between the bottom of the High Street and Church Street, you can see a section of walling which may be part of the original wall. The westward limits of the wall ran along the bottom of the burgage plots. Lawson Place and Monks Walk, off West Port, mark its line. The wall stood on the western side of these lanes, and between them and the bottom of the plots was an access way along which cattle could be driven out to the common pastures beyond. The wall was really more a boundary kept up by individual proprietors than a major line of defence.

Musselburgh

The name 'Musselburgh' is thought to have come from the beds of mussels which were found off the mouth of the River Esk. Although the town was founded much later than Edinburgh, the mussel beds perhaps account for the old rhyme:

Musselburgh was a burgh when Edinburgh was nane
And Musselburgh will be a burgh when Edinburgh has gane

The crossing place of the Esk, close to where it became tidal, was an obvious place for a town to develop. It was on the main road from Edinburgh to Berwick and the river crossing gave it strategic significance, as was shown by its role in the Battle of Pinkie in 1547 (Chapter 4). The importance of the estuary was appreciated by the Romans who built a fort at Inveresk (342719) just to the south of the town, on a high bluff overlooking the river. At that time the estuary may have been navigable for some distance above Musselburgh.

The town was created a burgh of barony under the abbey of Dunfermline between 1315 and 1328. In 1632 moves were made to promote it to a royal burgh. But the burgesses of Edinburgh, always paranoid about the possibility of a rival trading centre developing nearby, successfully blocked the plan. Musselburgh remained a dependent burgh with much of its industry and trade in the control of Edinburgh merchants. By late-medieval times the estuary has silted up so badly that it was difficult for shipping to reach the town and a new harbour was built at Fisherrow in the later sixteenth century.

The magnificent tolbooth at Musselburgh clearly embodies many features taken from the design of contemporary castles.

Musselburgh was an important textile-manufacturing centre. At the end of the seventeenth century a woollen manufactory employed several hundred outworkers in the town and the surrounding countryside. Fishing was also a major industry in the past although the harbour at Fisherrow now accommodates mainly pleasure craft.

Originally Musselburgh was only a single High Street along the main road. Its eastern end widens into an attractive market place with the tolbooth at one end and the grounds of Pinkie House at the other. The eastern end of the market place is marked by a pair of stone pillars bearing the burgh's coat of arms and dating from 1770. There are some attractive but unassuming seventeenth- and eighteenth-century houses around the market place but many of the older buildings have been replaced by modern ones, especially towards the western end.

The most prominent building in the main street is the tolbooth, one of the finest in Scotland, dating from about 1590 though its tower may be earlier. Local tradition claims that the tower was in existance in 1544 when it survived the destruction caused by the Earl of Hertford's army. The stone for building the tolbooth is said to have been obtained by dismantling the nearby chapel of Our Lady of Loretto. Like the Canongate tolbooth in Edinburgh, it has a fortress-like appearance and derives many of its features from contemporary tower-house architecture. Inside, the building is vaulted on all three floors and there is no direct connexion between the ground and first floors, save for the outside forestair, again emphasising the links with Scottish castles. A two-storey wing incorporating a council chamber was added in 1762.

At the eastern end of the town centre is Pinkie house, now part of Loretto School. Originally Pinkie House was a simple sixteenth-century tower belonging to the Abbey of Dunfermline, but it was greatly extended about 1613 by Alexander Seton, first Earl of Dunfermline. The old spartan tower was enlarged into an attractive mansion which incorporated new architectural ideas derived from England like bow windows, rusticated columns and a long gallery along with more traditional Scottish features like pepperpot turrets. Inside, Pinkie House has some fine painted ceilings from the early seventeenth century. The school takes its name from the sixteenth-century chapel whose stones were used for the tolbooth. Its former site is marked by a mound in front of the main school buildings. The original core of the school was an eighteenth-century house with later extensions. It became a school in 1829 and acquired Pinkie House in 1951.

The bridges across the Esk emphasise Musselburgh's importance as a staging post on what was once the 'Great Post Road' to Berwick. The oldest stone bridge was once popularly thought to have been built by the Romans but is more convincingly dated to the sixteenth century. It is an attractive three-arched bridge with a cobbled roadway and steps leading to it at either end; once there must have been ramps for wheeled traffic. The present structure may incorporate parts of the bridge which spanned the river at the time of the Battle of Pinkie in 1547 (Chapter 4). The bridge is likely to have been damaged either then or in the following year when English forces burnt Musselburgh, and tradition claims that it was rebuilt shortly after by Jane, Lady Seton. The modern road bridge was the work of the engineer John Rennie and dates

Loretto School, Musselburgh, on the site of a medieval chapel and incorporating the attractive old mansion of Pinkie House.

from 1806 although it has been widened more recently.

Musselburgh has no old burgh kirk: the town was served by the parish church of Inveresk half a kilometre to the south. Inveresk church stands on a raised site overlooking the river and adjacent to the Roman fort. There may have been a church here since the sixth century but the present surprisingly tall building dates only from 1805, replacing an earlier church which was built largely with stone and bricks from the Roman fort.

Musselburgh's early industrial history has left little trace apart from two eighteenth-century warehouses possibly tanning sheds, between the High Street and the river. In the nineteenth century a range of new industries developed including paper-making and the manufacture of fishing nets. The complex of mills and factories which housed these activites occupies the bend in the River Esk south-west of the town and makes an interesting collection for those interested in industrial archaeology.

All the excitement of a race day at Musselburgh.

Prestonpans

While Haddington and Dunbar were medieval burghs, Prestonpans was a late upstart whose fortunes were founded on coal and salt rather than on crafts and trading. Although it had been an industrial centre since the twelfth century, it was only created a burgh in 1552. Unlike other East Lothian towns Prestonpans developed from a series of small villages which grew together and eventually acquired the status of a burgh. One village was the fishing settlement of Aldhamer, later known as Saltpreston and then Prestonpans. Another was Preston, a short way inland. Preston now lies on the edge of the modern town, slightly aloof but preserving much of its old character. Closely grouped around the old mercat cross (Chapter 7) are an impressive tower house, Preston Tower (Chapter 3), two fine dovecotes, and two attractive early seventeenth-century mansions, Hamilton House and Northfield House (Chapter 6). It is difficult to visualise Preston as an important market centre but it was nevertheless here that the Guild of Chapmen, or pedlars, of the Lothians met annually until the later nineteenth century to elect their 'king'. From the sixteenth or early seventeenth century the focus of the settlement gradually shifted down to the coast. To the west

172

of Prestonpans was the village of Cuthill, which only merged with the burgh early in the present century when new housing filled in the open space between them. Cuthill was a salt and pottery-manufacturing centre too and there were many coal miners in the population as the collieries of Prestongrange and Prestonlinks were close by.

Although Prestonpans is best known for its coal and salt, fishing was also important. Oyster beds offshore were worked as well as more distant fishing grounds, and an annual Fisherman's Walk, similar to the one in Cockenzie, was held here, vying with the miners' gala as the main local event of the year.

Prestonpans has an attractive parish church, one of the first to be built in Scotland after the Reformation. It dates from 1596 but was enlarged in 1774. The south door and the west tower are from the original building and the churchyard has some fine old decorated tombstones. Inside the church there is an interesting painting, probably of eighteenth-century date, showing a naval vessel and fishing boats in a rough sea. It belonged originally to the local Fisherman's Society. The centre of the town is a single long street a short distance inland from the shore, with a rather straggling character. Early in the present century a writer described it as 'one continuous village of small houses, many of them ancient and all set down with grotesque rather than picturesque irregularity'. We would probably find this rather attractive today, but there has been a lot of modern re-development, some of it very attractive, though some of the older houses remain.

Cockenzie and Port Seton

Cockenzie grew up as a fishing and industrial centre around three small natural harbours. The most westerly has been converted into the modern Cockenzie harbour, the easternmost into Port Seton harbour. In between is the area known as the Boat Shore, quiet today but once a bustling fish market. When the fishing industry at Dunbar was in decline, early in the present century, Cockenzie was still thriving with over ninety deep-sea vessels. The Cockenzie fishermen and their families formed a distinctive little community. The women would walk westwards to the sands beyond Morison's Haven to dig for bait and, on their return, they would bait the hand lines for their men. The Cockenzie women were a canny bunch who normally kept the cash-boxes for the crews of the boats.

Their husbands were sometimes away for long periods, for Cockenzie vessels followed the herring shoals from their first appearance off southern Ireland in the spring, northwards through the Minch and then into the North Sea until, by the autumn, they were in local waters. By the third Friday in September they were usually back home. This was the date of the annual 'walk' or procession organised by the Friendly Society of Fishermen of Cockenzie and Port Seton. The night before the walk the children would build a bonfire at the Boat Shore and watch a firework display. At one time it was usual to build the bonfire round the hull of an old fishing boat.

Cockenzie was also a salt-making and mining centre, the salt pans being fired by the 'panwood' or small coal which was not fit for export. In the early seventeenth century the third Earl of Winton financed the building of Cockenzie harbour to facilitate the export of coal and salt from his estates. Later, in the eighteenth century, coal from the pits around Tranent was brought down to Cockenzie by waggonway (Chapter 10) and eventually by rail. Today coal is still brought in by rail, but instead of being exported it goes to the giant power station that dominates the western end of the town. Down to fairly recent times mining formed an alternative occupation to fishing, both of them hard and dangerous activities.

At the west end of the High Street is Cockenzie House, a later seventeenth-century mansion which may originally have been built by the Earls of Winton as the residence for the manager of their harbour and salt works. The warehouse beside it was probably used as a girnel for storing salt. Along with the rest of the Winton estates it was forfeited as punishment for the Earl's part in the Jacobite rebellion of 1715. It was bought by the York Buildings Company, a dubious group of financial speculators who did, at least, invest some money in this area by constructing the waggonway from Tranent to Cockenzie in 1722 (Chapter 10) and improving the harbour.

Subsequently the house was bought by the Cadell family. They were Cockenzie merchants who branched out into a variety of activities and made themselves a fortune in the process. In the mid-eighteenth century William Cadell teamed up with Samuel Garbett, a Birmingham businessman and manufacturer, and Dr John Roebuck, an Edinburgh chemist. Garbett and Roebuck had already set up a plant for manufacturing sulphuric acid as a bleaching agent for linen at Prestonpans in 1749 and it was here that they met Cadell. Cadell had the local contacts, Garbett the business acumen and Roebuck the technical knowledge. Together they founded the Carron Ironworks near Falkirk in 1759, the first Scottish ironworks to smelt iron ore using coal rather than charcoal. The ironworks might have been built at Cockenzie or Prestonpans. If this had happened the industrial development of this area during the later eighteenth and nineteenth centuries might have been very different and on a far larger scale. However, the iron ore that suited their processes best came from the Bo'ness area and Cadell was not able to negotiate sufficently favourable terms with local coal owners to make it worth their while bringing the ore to Cockenzie. Instead they opted for a site at Carron near the head of the Forth. The Cadells remained active in the Prestonpans area, though. In 1774 John Cadell bought the harbour at Cockenzie, the waggonway, and the collieries which it served. The family also replaced the old wooden waggonway with iron rails in 1815 and in 1835 they financed the building of a large new harbour at Cockenzie (Chapter 10).

Today Cockenzie still has some fishing, though the salt industry has vanished and mining has declined. Port Seton developed as a small-scale resort for day-trippers from Edinburgh, and its eastern end still has a rather ramshackle collection of huts, along with a large caravan park. The High Street still has some older houses with pantiled roofs among the more recent Victorian and Edwardian buildings.

North Berwick

North Berwick was founded as a burgh in 1373, belonging to the Earls of Douglas, and later became a royal burgh. In medieval times it was a staging point for pilgrims en route for St. Andrews. It also had a Cistercian nunnery, the remains of which can still be seen (Chapter 2). Nevertheless it remained a sleepy backwater. Because it was away from the main lines of communication, it never developed as a market centre in the way that Haddington and Dunbar did although it received some unwelcome notoriety in the late sixteenth century as the result of the North Berwick witch trials. In 1692 a report on the state of Scotland's royal burghs recorded that North Berwick possessed only two fishing boats.. In the nineteenth century, however, it became more significant as a fishing port. Like Dunbar, its dry and sunny climate encouraged visitors for sea bathing. In addition there were the attractions of fine sandy beaches, the striking cliff scenery eastwards towards Tantallon Castle, the offshore islands, notably the Bass Rock, and golf courses.

Inland the country rises towards North Berwick Law whose summit, on a clear day, is one of the most spectacular vantage points on the east coast of Scotland with the Firth of Forth and its rocky island laid out before you. It was only with the coming of the railway and the start of the tourist excursions and commuter travel that the settlement really began to develop. The prosperous late nineteenth-century villas which surround the town centre were architect-designed in a variety of styles and were occupied by professional people and businessmen from Edinburgh who commuted by train into the city.

The town is still clustered round its two small bays with the rocky headland between on which the harbour is built. The harbour is now a sleepy place once more with two attractive eighteenth-century warehouses beside it. At the corner of Quality Street and High Street stands the Town House, dating from the eighteenth century, with a clock tower and outside forestair. At the south end of Quality Street is the Lodge, once a town house of the Dalrymple family whose estate was just outside the burgh. The house has now been divided into flats but the grounds have been kept as a public park. North Berwick also has a museum in School Road which has exhibits relating to the history and wildlife of the area, as well as the history of golf.

CHAPTER 9

Mills, Mines and Manufactures

Even today with the development of power stations, suburban expansion, high-speed trains and trunk roads, East Lothian is a peaceful, predominantly rural area. But countryside does not necessarily mean just agriculture. For centuries the county has also been an important industrial area. Some industries, such as milling, brewing and textile manufacture, processed the products of local agriculture. Others like quarrying, lime burning and tile making provided raw materials for building the farmsteads, fertilising the fields and draining the land. There were also industries like coal mining, salt making and pottery which had no direct connexion with the land yet which were often found in the countryside. Because their scale of production was small these industries were able to co-exist with farming. Millers were often farmers themselves, while many farmers operated their own lime kilns and quarries. Textile manufacture also fitted in well with the slack periods of the agricultural year. Only from the later eighteenth century did the scale of some industries start to separate industry from its rural origins, either concentrating it in the towns or, in the case of coal mining, by creating new industrial landscapes.

Much of this industry has now gone, leaving only a few traces behind. The process of concentration and increasing scale of operation which drew industries from the countryside into the small towns sometimes ended by taking them to the cities and out of the county entirely or left only a single large cement works or quarry to take the place of the dozens of small ones which existed a century and a half ago.

This chapter looks at some of the old-established East Lothian industries and describes the remains of them which you can find throughout the county. Some sites, like Preston Mill, are widely known but others like the medieval coal heughs of Birsley Brae and the old limekilns which are scattered throughout the area are less publicised but equally interesting.

A corn-drying kiln at Preston Mill, near East Linton, may date from the 17th century and emphasises the need to dry the harvest in the fickle Scottish climate.

Mills and Milling

An industry found everywhere in East Lothian before the later eighteenth century was grain milling. Small grain mills, usually powered by water, were located close to every village and hamlet. There was generally at least one on every estate because milling was, like the possession of a doocot, a landowners' monopoly. There were nearly a hundred mills in East Lothian during the seventeenth century. Proprietors' feudal rights included thirlage – the right to compel their tenants to grind their grain at the estate mill. The landowner provided the capital for constructing the mill which was leased to a miller for a substantial rent. The miller recouped his rent by charging the tenants 'multures', a fixed proportion of the grain which they brought to be ground. Multures were usually set at about a twentieth of the ground meal or barley but could be higher. In addition to this payment the tenants were often required to provide labour for keeping the mill in repair and for bringing home new millstones. Millers were usually caricatured as rogues and cheats, and the records of many estates' baron courts suggest that there was often little love lost between them and the farmers within the 'sucken' or area within which all farms were bound to a particular mill. Although it was resented, so much thirlage was so profitable to proprietors that it was often not abolished until well into the eighteenth century.

Because each mill had a monopoly over a limited area there was little pressure for them to be efficient and their machinery was often simple in the extreme. Most of these old mills have long since disappeared, but Ordnance Survey maps often provide clues to their former location in place names containing 'Mill'. You can also find the remains of many old mills on the ground if you look for them carefully. A walk beside almost any East Lothian stream may reveal the overgrown foundations of a mill or traces of the mill lade. Not surprisingly, there was a string of them along the banks of the River Tyne. Between Haddington and East Linton, for instance, are the remains of Abbey Mill (534746), Sandy's Mill (551753), Beanston Mill (554754), Monk Mill (559751), and Hailes Mill (576758).

As thirlage was gradually abolished and milling became a more commercial occupation, these local mills declined. But a fine example has been preserved at Preston Mill near East Linton (595779). It has been restored to full working order by the National Trust for Scotland, and for a small fee you can have a guided tour of the machinery and learn about the intricacies of milling. The picturesque appearance of the mill buildings with their sandstone walls and red pantiled roofs makes them a favourite subject for artists and photographers. This emphasises how well such small-scale industries fitted into the life of the countryside before the Industrial Revolution. The River Tyne, which powered the mill, could be a fickle friend, though; as you go round the mill, look out for the marks which have been carved on the walls recording some of the more spectacular flood levels. The corn-drying kilns beside the mill were vital because the harvest was frequently late and the corn was brought in wet. The fabric of the mill itself

Poldrate Mill, Haddington. Originally a grain mill serving the burgh, its water wheel is still preserved.

probably dates from the eighteenth century but the kilns may be older.

Some interesting examples of a later generation of country mills also survive. Sandy's Mill, on the banks of the Tyne between East Linton and Haddington (551753), is later in date and larger than Preston Mill but it was still an estate mill serving the farms of the Kinlochs of Gilmerton. Much more spacious than Preston Mill, it is a three-storey building with a square brick kiln but retaining a traditional pantiled roof. It was used into the 1930s for making pot barley and grinding animal feed. At West Saltoun (469667) is another barley mill. It stands on the site of the first pot-barley mill in Scotland, built for Andrew Fletcher of Saltoun early in the eighteenth century (Chapter 5). The existing buildings seem to date to the later eighteenth century. Although the machinery of the mill has been removed, the L-shaped group of buildings, consisting of mill, granary and brick-lined kiln, is an attractive one.

Thornton Mill (742741) is also worth a visit. The buildings date from the late eighteenth or early nineteenth century but are nevertheless modest in scale, comprising only a single

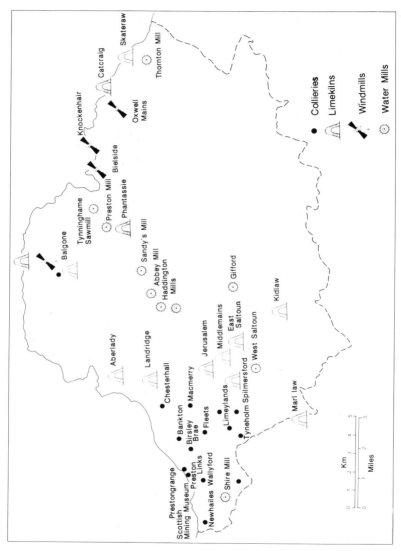

Map 13. Industrial Sites.

East Linton was an important milling centre in the 19th century as this old drawing of the mills beside the River Tyne show.

storey with an attic, and an attached kiln. The mill continued to operate into the 1960s before being converted to a knitwear factory and more recently to a private house. The wood and iron waterwheel, nearly five metres in diameter, has been preserved. It is an overshot wheel, the water being carried to the top of the wheel by a trough, rather than the undershot wheels turned by water at the bottom, which were cheaper to install and are normal for East Lothian mills.

Although most early East Lothian mills were water-powered, the low rainfall of the area and its gentle topography meant that it was not always easy to obtain a sufficient head of water to drive a mill wheel. Wind power was sometimes used as an alternative. It is not clear how many windmills were built in the county; probably only a few, but the remains of some of them can still be seen. At Knockenhair, on the outskirts of Dunbar (669789), you can see the tower of a seventeenth-century example which has been converted into part of a private house. The tower is still over five metres high and originally had a stone-vaulted room on the ground floor. Not far away at Bielside (655783) an even more substantial mill tower remains, nearly ten metres high and six metres in diameter. It too has been converted into a house. The windmill at Balgone Barns (553828), which probably dates from the late seventeenth century, has been less fortunate. It was converted to a doocot during the eighteenth century but is still impressive in its ruined state. Much more modest is a mill at Oxwell Mains (703763) which is only five metres high and was probably used for pumping water rather than for milling grain like the larger ones.

As thirlage declined and communications improved, milling became centred in the towns, particularly Haddington which has a fine collection of nineteenth-century mills along the banks of the Tyne south and east of the town centre. The largest group is Simpson's Maltings (514733) dating from the mid to late nineteenth century. The main building has four storeys and an attic with two kilns. Adjacent are the West Mills, flour mills dating from the 1840s but converted to tweed-making in 1885. The original mill block is four storeys high, and single-storey weaving sheds were added when it became a textile mill. The scale of this group of mills and maltings, when compared to Preston Mill, shows how much more commercialised agriculture and milling had become by the nineteenth century compared with a century or so earlier. Further downstream is Poldrate Mill (518734) on a site which has been occupied by mills since medieval times. Here you can see the three-storey mill with a kiln and steam-engine house, and linked to it across the road is a massive four-storey granary. The mill has been converted to a community centre but the original mill wheel has been preserved. Beside the Victoria Bridge are a further set of mills. Gimmers Mills (518740) stands on the site of earlier mills going back to the fifteenth century or earlier. The present buildings are mainly nineteenth-century, though, and were powered originally by a double water wheel.

Haddington was the largest grain market in Scotland until the coming of the railways caused milling, malting, brewing and distilling to be further centralised in the cities. Another legacy of this is the number of grain stores which survive in the town, most of them dating from the later eighteenth century or after. The finest of these tall buildings with their loading doors and hoists is 520738 but there are several other examples.

Brewing

Allied to grain milling in its direct links with agriculture was brewing, another old-established East Lothian industry. From the seventeenth century Dunbar, Haddington, Musselburgh and Prestonpans were all noted brewing centres. The Prestonpans brewery of John Fowler and Co. had a strong local clientèle for its famous 'Prestonpans Ale' among the fishermen and colliers but it was known throughout Scotland for its celebrated 'Wee Heavy'. During the 1960s Fowler's, like so many small independent breweries in Scotland, was taken over by a larger concern, in this case Allied Breweries. John Young and Company of Musselburgh were absorbed by Whitbread in a similar fashion. The small independent firms in Haddington have also closed though the buildings of Binnie's Brewery (519739), dating from the later nineteenth century, and a distillery (513734) from the same period, using earlier buildings which were once maltings, survive as a reminder of the industry.

Dunbar, whose harbour was a major exporter of grain, also attracted a number of brewing firms. James Boswell, passing through Dunbar on his way to London, considered the local brew to be 'the best small beer I ever had'. The local hard water, which is ideal for brewing, may have been one reason for the excellence of Dunbar's beer. Although there were various breweries in the town, the most famous is the Belhaven Brewery (665784). Founded in 1719 and still renowned for its real ales, Belhaven is one of the oldest breweries in Scotland. Brewing on this site has medieval origins, for during the thirteenth century monks from the Isle of May were granted land at Belhaven to provide food – and drink – for the monastery. Two of the wells which they dug still supply water to the brewery. The buildings of the brewery form an attractive group with sandtone rubble walls and red pantiled roofs. They date mainly from after 1814 when the original brewery was burned down, with additions after a further serious fire in 1887. The vaulted cellar is older and tradition links it with the medieval monks. Until the 1970s the main business of the firm was malting and they produced only about 150 barrels of beer a week for purely local consumption. The revival of interest in

G

real ale encouraged the firm to abandon the malting side of the business and concentrate on producing more beer.

One does not immediatly associate East Lothian with whisky making. The county has always produced large quantities of barley, though, especially from the lighter soils along the coast. The Glenkinchie Distillery (443668) has a name which sounds appropriate enough for a Speyside location, but in fact the Kinchie Burn flows into the Binns Water, a tributary of the River Tyne, south of Pencaitland. It was first established by a local farmer around 1840 but it produced only small quantities of whisky until 1886 when it was taken over by a Leith-based firm. In 1890 the name was changed to Glenkinchie – presumably because it had more of a Highland ring to it – and the present buildings were constructed.

Textiles

Before the Industrial Revolution every East Lothian village and hamlet had one or two weavers making coarse linen and woollen cloth from local flax and wool. Spinning the yarn was a common occupation for women as they sat around the fireside in the evening. Local families gave the yarn which they had spun to a weaver for making into cloth. These weavers worked purely for local markets, often only part-time. In the early phases of industrialisation spinning was mechanised first and the later eighteenth century was a period of prosperity for handloom weavers before this branch too went over to machine production. Although East Lothian was never a major cloth-producing area like Angus or Renfrewshire, several estate villages (Chapter 7) had clusters of weavers. Athelstaneford was noted for its coarse striped woollen cloth. Aberlady had over twenty weavers and its main street which is now disturbed by the noise of passing traffic formerly echoed to the regular clatter of their looms.

When John Cockburn had his new village of Ormiston built in the 1730s he laid out the first bleachfield in Scotland. Previously Scottish linen had been sent abroad for bleaching and finishing. Following the Union of 1707, however, it was possible to obtain premiums for establishing bleaching greens

Haddington's importance as a grain market is reflected in these modern maltings.

where the cloth, after an initial treatment with chemicals, was spread out in the open for several months in order to be bleached naturally by the sun. Another early bleachfield, belonging to the British Linen Company, was established at Saltoun in 1750. At one time it employed up to a hundred workers. When chemical bleaching became normal it was no longer necessary to tie up land on the outskirts of villages in this way. The bleaching green at Saltoun had been converted to a 'pleasure ground' by the end of the eighteenth century. At Gifford you can still see the site of the bleaching green, now a recreation ground, immediately west of the avenue from the centre of the village to Yester House (534678).

Even in the seventeenth century East Lothian had some larger-scale textile manufacture. Haddington was the site of a series of attempts to develop a woollen industry. The burgh, especially its suburb of Nungate, had the largest colony of weavers in the county so that there was a good deal of expertise in cloth-making here. A woollen manufactory and fulling mill was set up after the Scottish Parliament passed legislation to encourage the industry in 1641 and 1645 but it does not seem to have survived the occupation of the town by General Monck in 1651.

The buildings and land belonging to the manufactory, on what is now the Amisfield estate east of the town, were acquired by Sir James Stanfield and an Edinburgh merchant, Robert Blackwood. In 1681 the firm was re-established as the New Mills Company. The manufactory seem to have included a large three-storey building comparable in size with the early cotton mills of a century or so later. It was planned to have nearly 250 employees and to produce over 50,000 yards of cloth a year. Skilled workers and equipment were brought in from Yorkshire and the West of England to get the enterprise started.

The New Mills company concentrated on producing high-quality woollens, and at first they enjoyed a measure of success due to government backing. There was not, however, a large home market for fine woollens, and those who could afford such cloth tended to buy it from abroad. Legislation by the Scottish Parliament banning the import of foreign cloth had only a limited effect in helping the New Mills manufactory because foreign cloth was still smuggled in on a large scale. High tariff barriers gave the company some protection. The Haddington cloth was comparatively expensive to produce; a good deal of the best quality wool had to be imported because local wool was so coarse. They could not manage to produce fine woollens as cheaply as English manufacturers and for this reason they lost an important contract for army uniforms to an English competitor. The final blow was the customs union with England in 1707. The Union allowed cheap English cloth to flood the Scottish market and undermine the cloth from New Mills; the firm went out of business in 1711, only a few years later. Nevertheless, the New Mills manufactory survived for some thirty years during a difficult period for the Scottish textile industries. At the peak of production the firm employed up to 700 people, including outworkers scattered through the town and the surrounding country, and a sizeable village had grown up adjacent to the mill.

The demise of the New Mills company saw the end of the manufacture of fine woollens at Haddington, but the weaving of coarse woollen cloth continued, especially in Nungate. In

1750 a number of local clothiers and landowners combined to form the Tarred Wool Company of Haddington, an enterprise which bankrupted itself within a few years. Perhaps the name did not catch on with potential customers! It derived from the traditional practice of smearing sheep with a tarry mixture to protect them from weather and disease, a custom which did not improve the quality of the wool. Another firm set up later in the eighteenth century suffered a similar fate. In 1795 the factory buildings were converted for grinding indigo and other dyestuffs. The success of the Border woollen industry, particularly in the making of tweed, led to a new era of textile production in Haddington during the nineteenth century. In 1885 a former flour mill, West Mill (513734), was converted for tweed making. The mill itself was turned into a spinning factory and weaving sheds, which can still be seen were built alongside it.

In the eighteenth century East Lothian also had a number of lint mills for preparing flax. Although the linen industry was centred mainly in the west of Scotland, Angus, Fife and Perthshire, flax was grown widely and the Lothians still made a good deal of cloth. You can still see the remains of one of these mills at Grangehaugh (613752) on the Biel Water. It was built in 1750 for Lord Belhaven, a member of the Board of Trustees for Manufactures which was trying to encourage the linen industry. The mill, which seems to have been a substantial two-storey sandstone building powered by a water wheel, may have been built by Andrew Meikle the famous millwright (see Chapter 5). The dam for the mill a short way upstream of the bridge at Grangehaugh and the lade running from it to the mill are still visible as well as the ruins of the mill itself. The flax came from a wide area in the eastern part of the county and, despite the local decline in linen production, the mill continued to operate into the second quarter of the nineteenth century.

By the end of the eighteenth century the textile industry in East Lothian was being eclipsed by developments in other areas, notably the west of Scotland. Attempts to set up a cotton mill outside Dunbar were a failure and the industry was largely confined to some small-scale production of coarse cloth in places like Athelstaneford.

H

Coal Mining

Coal mining has been important in the west of the country since medieval times. The East Lothian coalfield is a small basin, separated from the larger Midlothian coalfield by an anticline, or arch of rocks, which forms the prominent line of hills south-east of Musselburgh. Within this basin the main seams are horizontal or dip only slightly. This, together with the fact that the seams are close to the surface in many places, meant that the coal was easy to reach and extract even by primitive mining techniques. The most important coal deposit, the Great Seam, which was up to seven feet thick around Tranent, was the closest to the surface. The seams were not broken up too much by faulting and drainage problems were not great. For these reasons coal was worked here at an early date and this area was Scotland's largest producer of coal during the seventeenth and eighteenth centuries.

The first recorded miners here were the monks of Newbattle Abbey who worked seams at Prestongrange during the thirteenth century. Mining had grown in importance by the sixteenth century. An account of the march of the English army through East Lothian in 1547 before the Battle of Pinkie (Chapter 4) tells how some English soldiers came across a coal pit with recent footprints at the entrance. Some local inhabitants had taken refuge by hiding in the pit. When one soldier ventured a little way into the mine, which must have been a horizontal level or adit, he was shot at by the refugees. The troops, evidently in an uncompromising mood, lit fires at the entrances to the pits to force the Scots to come out or be suffocated.

A major phase of expansion in mining occurred during the seventeenth century with the development of a substantial trade in coal to the Low Countries as well its increasing use in east-coast Scottish towns. The earliest workings had tapped seams which outcropped at the surface or lay only at a shallow depth. The coal was removed by sinking shallow pits down the surface and excavating for short distances around the bottom of the shaft. From their shape these workings came to be called 'bell pits'. When the coal had been extracted from around the shaft, or drainage problems were encountered, the pit was

Colliery pumping engine, Prestongrange. This engine is the centrepiece of the Scottish Mining Museum which houses a wide range of exhibits relating to the history of coal mining in Scotland.

abandoned and another one sunk. These early workings sometimes appear in the landscape today as slight circular hollows in the ground, and if you look carefully at the fields around Tranent and Ormiston you can see many depressions of this kind. The best example is at Birsley Brae just off the A1 west of Tranent (393729). Here in a small patch of woodland between the A1 and a minor road are the hummocky remains of a medieval coal 'heugh', now protected as an ancient monument. In summer the site is so covered with vegetation that it is difficult to see anything and the heugh is more easily seen in winter.

During the early seventeenth century a lot of investment in deeper workings was made by local landowners, notably the Earls of Winton whose prosperity was based largely on the profits from their mines. In order to work deeper seams it was necessary to install more effective drainage systems. This was done by cutting long drainage levels which came out at low points on the surface and drained the seams above. Some of these levels ran for miles underground and were the engineering wonders of their day. One which was planned at Elphinstone in 1623 was expected to take seven years to cut, and another at Pinkie took a year and a half to drive. The Earl of Winton's main level ran south to the Tyne Valley and still formed the basis of the system of mine drainage in this area in the nineteenth century. Another important level reached the surface at Bankton, north of Tranent.

If important progress in mine engineering was made during the seventeenth century, the same cannot be said for the conditions under which the colliers worked. So unpleasant was the job that it was difficult to recruit labour for the mines, and in 1608 the Scottish Parliament sanctioned the virtual enslavement of coal and salt workers and their families. From that time colliers could be bought and sold with the pits or moved from mine to mine at the whim of the proprietor, and were not allowed to leave their work without permission. In 1701 colliers and salt workers were even excluded from the Scottish equivalent of Habeas Corpus. Serfdom was not effectively abolished until 1799.

By this time conditions in the East Lothian mines were worse than in other parts of Scotland, due in part to the survival of old-fashioned working practices which had not been adopted in coalfields which had been developed at a later date. One feature of this was the large numbers of female workers. While men cut the coal, women were used to drag it to the shafts. Sometimes, where the seams were thin, they had to crawl through passages only two feet high, pulling their loads behind them. In the shallower pits they had to carry the coal to the surface as well. This involved climbing sets of wooden ladders with up to a hundredweight and a half on their backs. In the deeper mines the coal was wound up to the surface in tubs by horse gins where the animals walked round and round in a continous circle driving the machinery. Pregnant women often worked underground until they went into labour and returned to work within a few days of giving birth. Miscarriages were frequent and it was not unknown for women to deliver their babies in a field next to the pithead.

As well as women, young children were used to push truckloads of coal along the levels to the bottom of the shafts.

The work was hard, dangerous and degrading, leaving little time or energy for education or social life. A Parliamentary Commission in 1842 discovered children at Penston and Elphinstone collieries who had never been to church since baptism or attended a school. One of them, when asked about the length of the shifts that he worked, could not answer because he did not know what an 'hour' was. It was little wonder that the colliers and their families were a race apart. They lived in tight-knit communities, usually poorly housed, and often intermarrying. The hard physical work aged the young women dramatically, while silicosis killed off the men at an early age. Coal workers who survived into their fifties or sixties and were no longer fit for work were sometimes given a free house and an allowance of coal by the company but still lived in poverty, often making a small income from looking after the children of women who were working underground. As late as 1842 there were still 239 women and girls in the East Lothian mines, 35 of them under 13 years of age, as well as 53 boys under 13, with some children as young as six or seven. A Parliamentary Commission reported in 1842 that conditions in the East Lothian mines were worse than anywhere else in Britain, and in 1843 underground work for women and children was banned.

As the deeper seams were worked, the number of collieries fell and their size increased. In the early nineteenth century a large pit employed perhaps fifty colliers. A century later the biggest East Lothian mine, Prestonlinks Colliery, had over 1000 workers. The scale of coal production from each pit had grown even faster. In the 1860s, 100 tons of coal a day was considered a good output for a pit, but by the 1920s production of 1000 or even 1500 tons a day was being achieved. The 1920s and 1930s saw the peak of mining. From then the story has been one of steady rundown of production and closure of pits. Today coal mining has ceased, and fuel for the huge coal-fired power station which dominates Cockenzie is brought from Midlothian.

The centre of the mining area was Tranent, and even in the later eighteenth century a large proportion of the population of the town was employed, directly or indirectly, in the industry. Even more specialised were colliery villages where most of the workforce was employed in the mines. The miners were traditionally poorly housed, but from the later nineteenth century, and particularly after the First World War, the mining companies began to provide better housing. Good examples can be seen in mining villages like Elphinstone, Macmerry, Wester Pencaitland and Ormiston. With the closure of the pits many mining villages declined. Penston (446723) is a good example. It was once a large village but loss of employment when the local mines closed has caused it to shrink so that today only a farm and a handful of cottages remain.

Remains of the larger collieries are still prominent in the landscape. These include Fleets, south of Tranent (404712), Chesterhall near Longniddry (432752), Bankton near Prestonpans (397737), Limeylands and Tynemount near Ormiston (403694 and 402687), and Woodhall near Pencaitland (423687). There were also the two large coastal mines of Prestongrange and Prestonlinks (372736). In between them you can find remains of some of the smaller collieries which preceded them. Some of these are marked on large-scale Ordnance Survey maps but many are not. It should be stressed, however, that abandoned industrial sites like these can be dangerous and should only be explored with caution.

Although the pits have now closed and many of their surface traces have been cleared away, one superb monument to the industry still stands on the site of Prestongrange mine. This is a huge, brightly-painted beam engine, the only one of its kind left in Scotland. It was made by a Cornish firm for the Summerlee Iron Company who worked the Prestongrange mine. It was set up in 1874 and continued in operation until the mine closed in 1952. It was used for draining the pit: water was pumped out from the Beggar Seam, nearly 250m below the surface, in three stages by two engines at different levels underground and this one at the surface. The beam engine is encased in a tall, narrow engine house. Beside it are the remains of the later pithead baths. This site also has a line of kilns from the former Prestongrange Brick and Tile Works.

Together these features form the centrepiece of the Scottish Mining Museum. When the National Coal Board began to dismantle the surface buildings after the pit closed, various people including the former mine manager urged that they should be preserved as so many old collieries were being completely obliterated. They were too late to save the fine beehive kilns of the brickworks and many other features but the beam engine as well as the 24-chamber Hoffman brick kiln and its chimney were preserved. From small beginnings in the 1970s the museum has grown substantially. The former power station houses a collection of mining equipment. Outdoor exhibits include a shaft cage, examples of underground coal trucks or 'hutches', a steam crane of 1890 and colliery locomotives. The colliery canteen has been restored as an information centre with displays illustrating the history of mining in East Lothian. Here you can pick up leaflets describing a 'coal heritage trail' which runs through parts of East and Mid Lothian for 20km to the Lady Victoria Colliery at Newtongrange, taking in a variety of mining features from medieval to modern times. Much of the work in preparing and setting up the exhibits has been done part-time by enthusiasts, and every weekend you can find them there restoring engines and machinery.

Salt

One of the earliest of East Lothian's industries was salt manufacture. Salt making was important along the coast from Prestongrange to Cockenzie. The centre of the industry was at Prestonpans, whose name derives from the industry, as did its older one of Saltpreston. Salt was being made there as early as 1189 and continued for nearly 800 years. Producing salt by evaporating seawater in large iron pans was a byproduct of coal mining. Before the eighteenth century coal was mostly mined close to the coast because only water transport was sufficiently cheap for moving such a bulky commodity any distance. The large lumps, or 'great coal', were saved for export but the dross, or 'small coal', was used to heat the salt pans, hence its alternative name of 'panwood'.

The monks of Newbattle Abbey are thought to have started the industry here in medieval times, but it was only in the seventeenth century, with the expansion of coal mining, that salt making became big business. The third Earl of Winton, who was active in opening up coal mines on his estates, established a string of new salt pans along the coast. The pans were simply huge iron dishes. In the early nineteenth century they were eighteen feet long by ten feet wide but were only two feet deep. At high tide seawater was collected in ponds. Natural evaporation in these ponds made the liquid more saline and it was then transferred to the pans by buckets on the ends of poles. The industry was a profitable one: in the early seventeenth century salt was Scotland's third export, in terms of value, after wool and fish. The salt-making industry did not need a large labour force, though: only one man and a boy were needed to operate each pan.

Down to the eighteenth century much of the salt was exported but a lot was sold in Edinburgh too. The salt was carried there on the backs of women or 'saltwives' whose cry of 'Wha'll buy saut?' rang through the city's streets. Scottish sea salt was not as good a preservative as continental varieties because of impurities in the seawater, but despite this it was widely used because it was cheaper than imported salt. At the peak of production there were over twenty salt pans along this stretch of coast. In 1716-17 the salters of Prestonpans and district produced 67,400 bushels of salt, and by 1797-8 production had increased to 107,500 bushels. Over 90% of Scotland's salt came from the Firth of Forth, and over a third of this came from the Prestonpans area. So important was the salt trade that the question of imposing duties on it was an important issue in the debate leading to the Act of Union in 1707.

Thereafter, until the repeal of the salt duties in 1825, East Lothian salt had a measure of protection from foreign competition. Because customs duties were paid on it the salt was carefully locked away in storehouses or 'girnels' and guarded by the revenue men. A warehouse adjoining Cockenzie House and dating from the early eighteenth century may have been used as a salt girnel. Another example can be seen at Dunbar, near the harbour in Lamer Street. The industry declined from the early nineteenth century. After the repeal of the protective salt duties in 1825 foreign salt could be imported more cheaply while East Lothian salt also began to meet competition from Cheshire rock salt. The industry survived into the twentieth century in a small way, though, and the last pan ceased production as late as 1959. You can still see the works which belonged to the Scottish Salt Company in Prestonpans (385746).

Quarrying and Lime Burning

Like milling, quarrying was undertaken everywhere in East Lothian in the past. The red sandstones in the east of the county and the darker volcanic rocks of the country around Haddington provided good building stones and it was rarely necessary to look far for a suitable outcrop to quarry. Before the seventeenth century castles and churches were the principal stone buildings, and even in the towns most houses were of timber-frame construction with thatched roofs. From the seventeenth century the need for good building stone increased greatly. Stone was required for new harbour schemes, for road metalling, for making walls and enclosures, and increasingly for the houses of ordinary rural folk. Quarries were opened on an unprecedented scale and by the early nineteenth century most parishes had several. You can find the remains of them all over the countryside, their rock faces overgrown, the quarry-pits often filled with rubbish or sometimes water. They are rarely visited and should be explored with caution. Their abandoned condition shows how quarrying, like other industries in the county, changed from an activity which was carried on everywhere to one which was concentrated in a few locations. Today the most impressive quarry in the county is at the eastern end of Traprain Law (584750) whose volcanic rock provides excellent road metal. The quarry has virtually removed the end of the hill and has probably destroyed a lot of archaeological evidence of the prehistoric hill fort in the process.

While many quarries were opened for 'freestone', or bedded sandstone, for building purposes others worked limestone which was burnt for use as a fertilizer. The origins of agricultural liming in East Lothian go back to the early seventeenth century. At that time the benefits of spreading lime to neutralise soil acidity began to be appreciated. Probably the idea was introduced from England. Proprietors began searching for limestone on their lands, using coal or sometimes peat for burning it. There was a substantial increase in crop yields on farms which had ready access to limestone and coal, while a good deal of new land was also taken into cultivation in the west of the county. Some farms which had previously depended mainly on livestock were able to expand their area under crop dramatically with equally spectacular effects on the rents which they had to pay. They produced lime from primitive horseshoe-shaped 'clamp kilns'. These were simply built from turf and field stones, up to 12m long, 5m wide and 2m high. The coal and limestone were allowed to burn slowly for up to ten days and the kiln had to be virtually dismantled to extract the lime. None of these primitive kilns seem to have survived in this area, though examples are known from elsewhere in the Lothians.

This liming revolution only affected the west of the county because the poor state of the roads did not permit the transport of coal, or burnt lime, for more than a mile or two. The improvement of the roads in the later eighteenth century allowed virtually every lowland farm to use lime. By the later eighteenth century there was also increasing demand for lime for building projects within the Lothians, notably the building of Edinburgh's New Town, and the start of a thriving export trade.

The old clamp kilns were not suited to this greatly increased scale of production. A new kind of kiln, the more substantial vertical 'drawn kiln', was developed, and examples of them can still be seen throughout the county. They were built of stone but with an internal lining of brick, which resisted the heat more effectively. They were loaded from the top with alternate layers of coal and limestone. The burnt lime was taken out from the base and more rock and fuel were added from above. Access vents or 'draw holes' at the bottom allowed the removal of lime and production was virtually a continuous process. Single kilns are sometimes found but on many sites batteries of two kilns are common. They are usually built into a slope so that a horse and cart could be brought direct to the top of the kiln for loading the coal and limestone.

Once coal could be brought cheaply to almost any part of the county, lime could be quarried and burnt wherever it occurred. Figure 12 shows sites with surviving draw kilns. You can find limestone quarries and their associated kilns in some out-of-the-way places. A good example is at Kidlaw (509644), where a giant mass of limestone has been transported by ice sheets and dumped on top of a totally different bedrock. The quarry and limes kiln are still clearly visible. Other good examples of lime kilns in the western part of the county are near Gladsmuir (457754) and Saltoun (473692). At Rhodes, just outside North Berwick (572850), there is a substantial kiln. Local tradition claims that lime was exported from here to Ireland and that the ground in front of Rhodes farmhouse has been formed by ballast from Irish vessels. Another well-preserved lime kiln stands at Phantassie, near East Linton (602768).

Limestone also occurred south of Dunbar, but without any local coal for burning it. Coal was brought in by sea and the little harbour at Skateraw (739754) was specifically constructed by local farmers for this purpose. A lime kiln is still visible by the shore. The burnt lime from Skateraw was bought by farmers from the Berwickshire Merse, who had no local limestone. They brought their carts over the moors and through the gorge of the Pease Burn to Skateraw, making the difficult return journey to their farms fully laden. Sometimes as many as 300 carts might be waiting to load lime from the kilns. Lime was also exported by sea to the Devon Iron Works in Clackmannanshire. Another set of coastal lime kilns in this area has been preserved at Catcraig, just south of Dunbar (715773). The kilns continued in use until 1921 and have been restored with notice boards explaining how they worked. There is one double kiln and a battery of three, as well as the remains of a gunpowder store. The lime-making tradition is still carried on at East Barns near Catcraig by a huge modern cement works whose size helps put the scale of the eighteenth-century industry into perspective.

Pottery and Tile Making

Even in medieval times pottery manufacture was important in East Lothian. At Colstoun (520709), south of Haddington, medieval pottery kilns have been excavated and a vast quantity of sherds discovered around them and in nearby fields. These sherds were mostly the potters' 'throw-outs', from vessels which had been badly fired. The pottery appears to date from the thirteenth century and closely resembles 'Scarborough Ware' from Yorkshire which was traded to many places in eastern Scotland in the days of peace with England before the Wars of Independence. Colstoun Ware has, not surprisingly, turned up in nearby Haddington but also at Gullane, North Berwick, Tantallon Castle, and further afield at Coldingham, Edinburgh, and the abbeys of Melrose and Jedburgh.

In later times the coast between Prestonpans and Musselburgh was noted for pottery making, and if you rummage around some of the old factory sites you can still find plenty of broken sherds. The most famous of the early Prestonpans potteries was founded by William Cadell. Cadell's father was a Haddington merchant who moved to Cockenzie about 1730. From general trading William expanded his interests. He teamed up with Samuel Garbett, a Birmingham businessman, and Dr. John Roebuck, a brilliant chemist. The trio founded a chemical works and soap factory at Prestonpans but they were also interested in pottery. Cadell and Garbett established a pottery works here in 1751 for making stoneware, a near-white pottery which was glazed using local salt and fired with local coal. The pottery was located just west of the parish church (388746).

They also made better-quality pottery known as creamware, similar to Staffordshire ware, with a creamy-white colour. This was made from Devon clay mixed with ground flints which were imported via Morison's Haven. If you hunt around the sites of some of the potteries you can still find nodules of this flint, which does not occur in the local rocks. The water mills at Acheson's Haven which worked by tidal power and had first been built in the later sixteenth century for grinding grain were, by the end of the eighteenth century, grinding flint for the pottery industry instead. The Cadells also used a flint mill on the coast north of Seton Church (416759). Although the mill has gone, you can still pick up flint in the neighbourhood. Much of the creamware from the Cadells' pottery was exported to countries ranging from Russia to Sicily. Comparatively little pottery from the Cadell works has survived, but the Chambers Street branch of the Royal Museum in Edinburgh has some fine examples.

Cadell's nephew, also called William, left the business in 1764 and set up his own pottery at Bankfoot on the western side of Prestonpans. His house later became a Miners' Welfare Institute (378741), and the pottery was located where the nearby bowling green now stands. Another pottery making salt-glazed stoneware was sited at West Pans (364733). Although there are only a couple of cottages here today, this was once a thriving village with over 300 inhabitants. Fragments of pottery can still be picked up on the beach nearby. The clay was obtained locally from the grounds of the Drum Mohr estate, and the remains of the old clay pits can still be seen (365732). The industry continued producing coarse white and brown 'stoneware' into the early part of the twentieth century. Although individual potteries had their ups and downs, the industry survived in this area down to the First World War. You might like to look for later examples of pottery from this area in antique shops and at sales. One of the most familiar products was a type of glazed brown teapot known locally as 'Broon Coos'.

A more widespread industry was tile manufacture. The attractive pantiles which roof so many of East Lothian's older buildings are thought to have been brought originally from the Low Countries as ballast. Unlike more conventional ballast, they could be sold at a profit along with the cargo! Local firms, notably one at Musselburgh, began making them towards the end of the eighteenth century. In the first half of the nineteenth century the other major demand for tiles was for field drainage. Undersoil drains had long been advocated by agricultural improvers, but only when a machine had been invented for mass-producing hollow tiles with a standard bore did large-scale drainage of this kind became feasible. Several estates established tile works. On the Saltoun estate a brick and tile factory set up in 1834 had turned out over half a million drainage tiles within a decade. Some shrewd farmers got in on the act too. George Hope, who leased the farm of Fentonbarns south of Dirleton, set up his own kiln for making drainage tiles. He produced enough to supply his neighbours as well as for his own needs. The profits from selling the surplus tiles paid for the installation of drains on his own farm!

At Prestongrange the remains of a large brickworks can still be seen. Here the raw material was not clay dug at the surface but 'fireclay', a deposit which occurred below ground between the coal seams and was mined along with them. This clay was used to produce heat-resistant bricks for the interiors of kilns and ovens, as well as normal building bricks. The company exported its bricks and tiles to Denmark, Holland and Germany, using the harbour of Morison's Haven until the First World War.

CHAPTER 10

Highways and Byways, Harbours and Havens

When you explore an area like East Lothian, it is easy to take the roads, from farm track to trunk road, for granted without thinking about their age or how they have helped to shape the landscape. The history of routeways and tracks in this area, and probably harbours too, goes back to man's first appearance but, inevitably, most of what is visible today relates to the most recent periods of heaviest use. Nevertheless,, by studying routes on the map and following them on the ground you can reconstruct a good deal of the history of transport in East Lothian over the last few centuries.

By contrast with road transport, which was rarely documented in any detail because everyone took it for granted, railways came late and are well recorded. Yet, apart from the main east-coast line and the branch to North Berwick, the age of the train in East Lothian has passed. Following abandoned railway lines can be as interesting as walking old roads. It is easy to forget the importance of the sea as a means of transport and source of livelihood in the past, for in East Lothian today the sea generally means recreation and leisure rather than work. The string of harbours from Fisherrow to Skateraw is a reminder of this past importance. There are no large harbours, although in the early nineteenth century it was once proposed to extend the one at Dunbar so that it could shelter an entire fleet. As a result they have preserved much of their old atmosphere.

Old Bridges

In East Lothian there were no purpose-built roads outside the towns before the mid-eighteenth century. Roads were worn by use rather than constructed, and even the important route from Edinburgh to Berwick was merely a broad band of interconnected tracks which only narrowed where the line of travel was more clearly demarcated by the policy walls of an estate or by the need to cross a river. While road maintenance

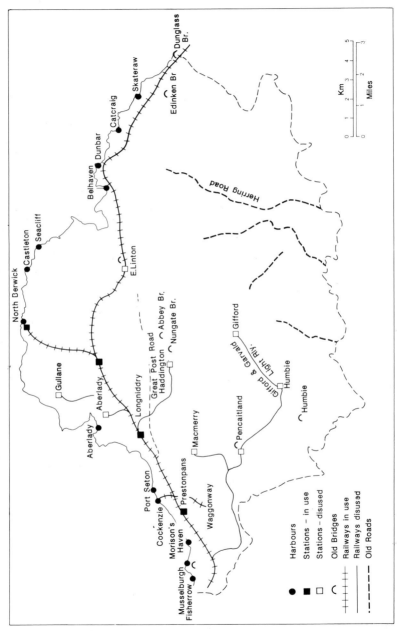

Map 14. Old Roads, Railways and Harbours.

The Victoria Harbour at Dunbar, now quiet, was once the busiest in East Lothian. In the foreground is the lifeboat *Herbert Leigh*.

was perfunctory, the importance of the main routes at least is shown by the fine bridges which have survived. In late-medieval times most bridges were probably of timber, but during the sixteenth century a number of stone ones were built on the Edinburgh to Berwick road and at other places across the Tyne, the only river in East Lothian which presented a major obstacle to traffic.

Close to the line of the modern A1 there is a fine sixteenth-century bridge at Musselburgh (343728). It was probably built, or rebuilt, in the 1550s, perhaps as a replacement for one destroyed in 1548 by the English garrison at Haddington when they burnt the town (Chapter 4). The steps which lead up to the three-arched bridge are a late addition; originally there were ramps for carts and animals. At East Linton (592772) the old bridge was probably built at a similar date to the one at Musselburgh but it has been frequently repaired so that the upper parts date from the later nineteenth century. The site of this bridge, above the rocky falls of the Tyne, is particularly attractive. The Nungate Bridge over the Tyne at Haddington

(519738) also dates from the sixteenth century but was extensively repaired during the eighteenth century when further arches were added at its eastern end to reduce the steep gradient. Another old bridge over the Tyne near Haddington is Abbey Bridge (533746) with three arches dating from the early sixteenth century but repaired at least twice subsequently to judge by inscribed panels in the stonework. The oldest of all the bridges still in use is probably the one over the Tyne at Pencaitland (442690) which bears the date 1510 and the arms of the Sinclairs on one side. Of old bridges over smaller streams the simple, single-arched example at Humbie Mill (462630), dating from the seventeenth century, is one of the most attractive.

The Great Post Road

The most important route through East Lothian was the one from Edinburgh to Berwick. This was the main stagecoach route through the county from 1678 when the first coach service from Edinburgh to Haddington was started. A regular letter post between Edinburgh and Berwick was established in 1635 although the service was not always reliable. Apart from robberies the mail was delayed by various accidents. In 1733, for instance, the mail was delayed because the drunken post-boy fell off his horse which promptly bolted with the letters. The following year both mail and rider were lost in the River Tyne.

For parts of its course the great post road followed the line of the modern A1. However, the old road had two branches, one which passed through Haddington and Tranent, and another which ran further to the north. Sections of this northern route have been almost abandoned by modern traffic and can be walked or cycled in safety. From Cantyhall (434752), 1km south-east of Longniddry, the road runs eastwards as a minor farm track for over 7km until it reaches Phantassie (510757) north of Haddington. Although the road itself is a modern metalled one, it follows the course of the old road closely. If you look at the 1:25,000 map you will see that its gently sinuous course contrasts sharply with the later, right-angled pattern of fields on either side. From Phantassie eastwards for 3km the road vanishes although a curving field boundary probably preserves its original course. From Beanston Mains (553765) the road continues as a cart track to Pencraig Wood (569765). If you look where the modern track turns at the north-west corner of the wood, you can see a short section of the old road itself, in the form of a deeply worn hollow way, running into the trees.

The Edinburgh to Berwick road was important as a through route but was also vital to local farm traffic. It is indicative of the early start to agricultural improvement in the county that this was the first road in Scotland to be made into a turnpike by parliamentary act in 1750. Previously this and other roads in East Lothian had been maintained by the old statute labour system whereby able-bodied men were required to turn out for six days a year with their own horses, carts and tools to help repair the roads. Needless to say the labour was given grudgingly, the work was unskilled, and the results were poor. The turnpike trust employed professional engineers and surveyors to upgrade the road and recouped their investment by levying tolls on traffic. If some people, like the inhabitants of Haddington, objected to having to pay a toll on every load of coal brought from the pits at Tranent, it was soon evident that the new system made a vast improvement in the speed and cost of traffic. By the end of the eighteenth century the turnpiking of some of the county's other main roads was well in hand. Road transport was now mainly by cart instead of by pack horse, as had been normal in the middle of the century. Where formerly it had taken a full day to travel by coach from Haddington to Edinburgh, the journey could now be made in two and a half hours and the people bringing the coal from Tranent to Haddington could make between four and six round trips a day instead of merely one.

The main A and B class roads through the county still mostly follow the routes of the late-eighteenth and early-nineteenth turnpikes, but modern metalling and road widening make it difficult to appreciate what the turnpikes were like. Some turnpike toll houses have survived, though, to recall this important era of road construction. They were usually single-storey slate-roofed cottages with windows strategically placed so that the toll collector could keep an eye on traffic in both directions. A good example of a toll house survives at the west end of Aberlady (462798) and another near Haddington (515745). Other tolls around Haddington are commenorated by places names such as Blackmains Toll on the old line of the great post road (502757) and Abbey Toll (531752).

Old Roads in the Lammermuirs

Following a modern farm track on the line of an old road is not as interesting as looking for abandoned sections of the original roads themselves. There is little scope for this in the lowlands as the landscape has been so thoroughly altered since the eighteenth century. The best place to look for old roads is in the Lammermuirs where many of them can be followed for miles. You can combine the exploration of one old road with a walk to the summit of Lammer Law, one of the highest points in the county (a round trip of about 7km with an ascent of 300m). If you leave your car at Longyester (545652) a track leads south-eastwards towards the hills. It follows an old routeway which ran south from Haddington and crossed the Lammermuirs to Lauderdale. Once you have climbed to the top of Brown Rig (537634) you start to find traces of older roads underlying the modern track. Two deeply-hollowed tracks cut through the summit of the hill. If you continue to follow the modern cart track south-eastwards you come to a long climb up the northern slope of Threep Law (530627). This slope is criss-crossed by a band of intertwining hollowed trackways.

Old roads like these generally appear as hollows on level, firm ground or on moderate slopes. On steeper ground they tend to climb in zigzags, forming terraces in the hillside which are often embanked at their outer edge. These roads were worn by repeated traffic, not deliberately made, and the swathe of tracks on Threep Law shows how each rider and carter chose his own line of ascent. The band of tracks narrows higher up as the road skirts around the steep drop into the valley to the east. Once on top of the broad plateau of Lammer Law, traces of these tracks tend to fade out in the peat. It is difficult to date remains like these as they probably represent

Cockenzie harbour, dominated by the power station, still continues its fishing traditions though on a much smaller scale than formerly.

the accumulated wear of centuries and the routes remained in regular use until well into the nineteenth century.

The Lammermuirs are criss-crossed with old trackways of this type. A particularly good example which is readily accessible lies close to the modern B6355 road from Gifford to Duns. A broad band of intertwining trackways climbs up the north slope of Newlands Hill from 589657 to join the modern road at 596654. The belt of tracks is up to 150m wide, and in places it is possible to distinguish up to sixteen separate hollow ways, some of them flat-bottomed and probably cut by the passage of carts and sleds, others V-sectioned and deepened by recent erosion. A little further south, where the modern road skirts the head of the Papana Water, further tracks cut as terraces into the hillside can be seen on either side of the road, especially downhill (600650). A road on this line is mentioned in a thirteen-century charter relating to lands held by Melrose Abbey. The tracks have evidently been cut by prolonged use but like the route over Lammer Law have been used into the eighteenth century if not later and their present appearance probably reflects comparatively recent traffic.

This ancient road is paralleled and in places overlain by a modern one partly because it follows an obvious pass over the Lammermuirs. Other old roads connecting East Lothian with Lauderdale and the Merse take routes which no modern roads have used. Although less accessible, they make interesting cross-country walks and, because they are only followed by rough farm and moorland tracks, it is possible to get a better impression of their original character. One of these lost roads climbs from Stoneypath (616711) and Moorcock Hall (616702), south of Stenton, and runs over Dunbar Common down to the old fortified house of Johnscleuch (631664). On either side of the modern track traces of older roads can be seen. From Johnscleuch the road crosses the slopes of Nine Stone Rig (630656) as a belt of hollow ways. Beyond the Kingside Burn traces of the road vanish in the improved ground around Mayshiel (624642) but continue southwards across the Fasney and Dye Waters towards Westruther.

Another old road through the Lammermuirs is the 'Herring Road' from Dunbar to Lauderdale. As the name suggests, this route was used in the seventeenth and eighteenth centuries by the inhabitants of Lauderdale for bringing home supplies of herring for the winter from Dunbar. The line of the road climbs from near Spott over Lothian Edge, the northern escarpment of the Lammermuirs (Figure 13). From 658716 a broad band of old hollow ways can be seen on either side of the modern track. The road crossed the Whiteadder south of Johnscleuch (638658), and continued south-eastwards by the head of the Dye Water towards Lauderdale.

Harbours and Havens

Today East Lothian seems primarily an agricultural area and it is easy to forget how important the sea has been in the past as a means of communication and a source of livelihood. Despite this the county has always suffered from the lack of good large natural harbours. The coastline provides a number of rocky creeks and some sheltered bays and estuaries but few harbours of any size. Before the nineteenth century this did not matter so much because fishing and cargo vessels were small and could operate from havens which were little better than open beaches. There are no traces of any harbour works at Thorntonloch (755744) south of Dunbar or Tyninghame (625793) although they are mentioned as being used by shipping in the late seventeenth century. The coming of the railways and the concentration of trade in fewer large ports, together with the decline of the fishing industry, has meant that many of the county's small harbours have been largely abandoned. This also means that they have not been altered by recent port developments so that there is plenty of scope for exploring them and trying to discover what they were like in the past.

It is often the smallest and simplest harbours which are the most fascinating. At Castleton (594850) below the cliffs on which Tantallon Castle stands there are traces of a landing place which may have served a small fishing community as well as the castle itself. Just below the west corner of the castle bailey is an area of flat rocks whose surface is pitted with depressions which probably represent the post holes for a former landing stage whose date is uncertain but which was probably contemporary with the period during which the castle was in use – from the fourteenth century to the seventeenth. Beside the remains of the landing stage is a channel in the rocks up to 10m wide which seems to have been deliberately cleared of boulders to provide an anchorage for small vessels. Nearby at Seacliff (602847), adjacent to the ancient centre of Auldhame, a rectangular basin about 20m long has been cut out of the rocks. Although the site has some similarities with Castleton and may have been used at an early date, the cutting of the rock seems comparatively fresh and, while nothing is known about the construction of this little harbour, it is possible that it dates from the nineteenth century and was associated with nearby quarries.

Another lost haven is Aberlady which once had the distinction of being the official port for Haddington. Haddington, although an inland town, was a royal burgh and so had the right to engage in overseas trade. However, it required an outlet to the sea, and an early charter granted in Aberlady. Visiting Aberlady today and looking across the silted estuary of the Peffer Burn to the salt marshes and sand dunes on the Gullane side it is hard to visualise it as a thriving port.

Indeed there is no evidence of any artificial harbour works here and it seems that vessels merely anchored in the open estuary. The mouth of the Esk at Musselburgh is equally unpromising as a haven today but the estuary was used as a port from medieval times and it seems likely that it has gradually silted up over the centuries. An attempt at building a proper harbour was made in the early eighteenth century but results seem to have been disappointing and attention was transferred to Fisherrow, a kilometre to the west, where a small harbour was begun in 1743. Although it has been suggested that the Esk might once have been deep enough to allow vessels to come right up to the old bridge near the heart of the town, the lack of a proper harbour is likely to have hindered Musselburgh's development.

Other harbours were built by local landowners to allow them to export the agricultural produce and mineral wealth of their estates. A good example of this on a small scale is Skateraw (738754). The rocky creek here was used as a landing place in the sixteenth century and probably earlier, but it was developed during the early nineteenth century when it was realised that the local limestone could be burnt to produce agricultural lime. Two local landowners, Brodie of Thorntonloch and Lee of Skateraw, had a small harbour built with a lime kiln beside it. The harbour is now derelict and silted up, having been destroyed by a storm during the late nineteenth century, and a gravel beach has been thrown up in front of the kiln, destroying or burying the old quay.

The earliest instance of a landowner sinking capital into harbour construction was at Morison's Haven (372738) where the monks of Newbattle Abbey received permission to build a harbour on their Prestongrange lands early in the sixteenth century. It is not clear how much they achieved, but it is likely that they sub-contracted the work, for in 1541 Alexander Acheson was granted the land for the purpose of constructing a harbour which became known as Achieson's Haven. A later landowner, William Morison, reconstructed the harbour on a larger scale around 1700 and the port then became known as Morison's Haven. It served as the main harbour for the thriving coal and salt town of Prestonpans but reclamation of the foreshore has now filled it in and little is visible of the piers.

A larger-scale undertaking financed by a private landowner was the harbour of Cockenzie (398756). The piers there were built by the Earl of Winton in the 1630s to enable him to export coal and salt from his estates. Despite storm damage later in the century the harbour continued in use and was refurbished by the York Buildings Company in 1722 when they constructed the waggonway from Tranent to the harbour (see below). The harbour was bought by the local industrialist John Cadell in 1774 and was completely rebuilt for him to a design by the engineer Robert Stephenson. The new harbour was completed in 1833 and, although designed primarily for exporting coal, it also had a flourishing fishing industry.

Dunbar has been the most important East Lothian harbour for several centuries despite its small size and problems of access. The earliest harbour was at Belhaven (662784) to the west of the town where Belhaven Bay is sheltered from easterly gales by the promontory on which Dunbar stands. Belhaven was being used as a harbour in 1153, and in 1369-70 when the Earl of March was granted the right to found a burgh this was its official harbour. The building of a proper harbour among the rocks at Dunbar started in 1574. In 1655 a storm ruined the harbour works and the burgh petitioned for financial aid to reconstruct it. A sum of money, supposedly £300, was contributed by Cromwell's government for this purpose. The foundations of the present east pier probably date from the sixteenth century although it is sometimes suggested that it was first built in Cromwell's time.

The old harbour had reached its present form by the mid-eighteenth century with an extension to the east pier dividing the inner harbour from Broad Haven. Much of the character of the harbour today is due to the old buildings which surround it. The warehouses at the foot of Victoria Street are particularly attractive although the custom house which stood nearby has been demolished. On the short pier at the mouth of the harbour is Spott's granary, a three-storey red sandstone building which is first recorded in the early years of the eighteenth century and may be older. The building has been converted into flats with some attractive new houses in traditional style built alongside. Its presence is a reminder that grain was the harbour's major export item in the past. Other granaries and maltings dating from the eighteenth and nineteenth centuries stand around the harbour. To the north-west of the Old Harbour is the larger Victoria Harbour, built in 1842, with a sea wall linking two offshore rock outcrops. On Lamer Island to the north of the Old Harbour there are the remains of a battery of sixteen cannon built by the town after Captain Fall, an American raider, had tried to capture a ship moored in the harbour entrance. The battery was provided with a furnace to allow the roundshot to be fired red hot so that they might set attacking vessels on fire. After the end of the Napoleonic wars the battery was converted into a hospital and continued to be used for this purpose until the First World War.

During the seventeenth and eighteenth centuries Dunbar was the foremost centre of the herring fishery in eastern Scotland. By the end of the eighteenth century the trade had declined drastically. For a time a whaling company, the East Lothian and Merse Fishing Company, financed mainly by local landowners, operated out of Dunbar, exploiting the waters around Greenland.

North Berwick has another old harbour. Although never as important as Dunbar, with less foreign trade and fishing, the harbour here is at least as ancient. A natural harbour is formed by the promontory on which fragments of the old church of St. Andrew stand, and a reef of rock running to the north-west of this. This was in use as early as 1177 for the crossing of pilgrims to St. Andrews (Chapter 2), but it is not clear at what date a proper harbour with piers and breakwaters was constructed. The pier at the inner end of the harbour is recorded in the early eighteenth century and may be older, but the rest of the habour dates from the late eighteenth and nineteenth centuries. A severe storm in 1811 damaged much of the existing structure and necessitated major repairs. Two fine eighteenth-century warehouses stand near the harbour, one of them now converted into flats.

Railways

The first railway in East Lothian – one of the earliest in the world – was a colliery waggonway from pits at Tranent to the sea at Cockenzie. It was built in 1722 by the York Building Company, a rather dubious group of developers who bought the Earl of Winton's estates after they had been forfeited following the Jacobite rebellion of 1715. The original waggonway had wooden rails with a gauge of three feet three inches. The waggons trundled downhill under gravity with a brake-man to control their speed, and were hauled back by horses. It was later converted to iron rails by the Cadells of Cockenzie. The course of the waggonway can still be traced today, cutting under the main road through Tranent (402729) and descending the steep slope to the north through a gully known locally as the Heugh. The line of the waggonway has been landscaped into an attractive walk leading from the centre of Tranent to the old parish church.

Although Sir John Hope built another short waggonway at Pinkie in 1767, the first railway to use wrought-iron rails, the early development of railways using steam locomotives occurred on the inland coalfields of north Lanarkshire. It was not until plans were well advanced for a railway linking Edinburgh and Glasgow that the idea of a line from Edinburgh through East Lothian to Berwick and beyond was first seriously mooted. Plans for a line linking England and Scotland via a west-coast route were in vogue and it proved difficult to interest either Scottish or English investors in an east-coast line. In 1844, however, Parlimentary approval was granted for a line from Edinburgh to Berwick, and the North British Railway was born. It was the plan of the founder, John Learmouth, to annexe a huge triangle of country between Edinburgh, Berwick and Carlisle, but like so many early railway promoters he was unduly optimistic about the traffic which would be generated in this largely agricultural area with few towns or mineral resources.

Construction of the main line to Dunbar provided few engineering problems as gradients were gentle, although a bridge over the Esk at Inveresk and another over the Tyne at East Linton were required. Looking at the railway on the modern map, it may seem strange that the line runs north of the Garleton Hills rather than south, through Haddington. At this early stage in railway history engineers still tried to avoid obstacles rather than buiding embankments, cuttings and tunnels. The engineer who advised Learmonth suggested that to route the railway through Haddington across the higher ground east of Tranent would add substantially to the construction costs and also to the long-term maintenance of the line. The solution adopted was to build a branch line to Haddington, whose inhabitants seem to have been in two minds about the coming of the railway. Some welcomed it but others prophesied, correctly, that it would ruin Haddington's position as the largest grain market in Scotland once farmers could deal directly with Edinburgh and Glasgow.

Beyond Dunbar the character of the line changed, with some difficult streams such as the Dunglass Burn to bridge and a steep climb over the fringes of the Lammermuirs to Grantshouse. Nevertheless, the railway was opened in June 1846 and stagecoach services on the main road through the county were immediately abandoned in the face of competition from five through trains a day from Edinburgh to Berwick. However, heavy rain during the following autumn showed up the defects in construction due to jerry-building contractors. The bridges at East Linton and at Beltondod, near Dunbar, collapsed and elsewhere along the line embankments were washed away. A good deal of money had to be spent on hurried repairs before the line could be re-opened.

Given that the line ran through a mainly agricultural area, Learmonth was misguided in having too many unprofitable branch lines constructed. The one to Haddington was originally built as a double track, partly from fear of competition from the East Lothian and Tyne Valley Railway, which was intended to run from the North British line at East Linton via Haddington to Ormiston and Dalkeith but which, in the event, was never built. Traffic on the Haddington branch never came up to expectation and the line was later reduced to a single track. Another branch from Drem to the as yet undeveloped village of North Berwick, with an intermediate station at Dirleton, was also built for double tracks although only a single line was ever laid. The company had high hopes

Mending the nets at Port Seton harbour.

of generating traffic by encouraging Edinburgh businessmen to live in North Berwick and commute into the city. They did this by offering concessionary 'line of residence' tickets to people with businesses in Edinburgh who had a house built within a specified radius of one of their stations. In the long term North Berwick did develop as a commuter settlement and holiday resort but the company were slow to recoup the initial cost of the line. In 1856, only six years after the branch opened, revenue was so poor that they abandoned locomotives and resorted to horse power on the line to reduce running costs. A branch line to Tranent was more successful as there was a good deal of traffic in coal, but the North British so overextended themselves in building unprofitable branch lines here and in the Merse that they had insufficient funds to maintain their engines and rolling stock properly, so for a while the railway was notorious for its frequent breakdowns.

Later in the nineteenth century East Lothian acquired other branch lines. The Aberlady, Gullane and North Berwick Railway attempted to build a more direct line along the coast to North Berwick but the line, which was opened in 1898, got no further than Gullane. This helped turn Gullane into a resort and golfing centre, and the golf course at Luffness even had its own private platform.

The last new line, and in many ways the most curious, was the Gifford and Garvald Light Railway, which started from Ormiston but never got beyond Gifford. The line was opened in 1901 right at the end of the railway era. It ran through thinly populated countryside with few mineral resources, and indeed the line (Figure 13) actually avoided villages like East and West Saltoun. The area south of Haddington, despite the improvement of the local roads in the nineteenth century, was still relatively isolated. The line was promoted by local landowners hoping to open up markets for their agricultural produce and minerals. Authorisation for the railway had been granted as early as 1891 but squabbles between the directors and the proprietors involved in promoting the line delayed its opening. One landowner, Fletcher of Saltoun, withdrew his co-operation and the line had to be re-routed in a big sweep south to avoid the main part of his estates.

The Gifford and Garvald line was classified as a light railway, specifically designed to serve rural areas with limited traffic and built and run more cheaply as a result; it was very much a second-rate railway. The level crossings on the line were unmanned; the train had to stop at them while the guard got down and opened the gates. The speed of the trains was severely restricted and the stations were very basic in their facilities. The line had small hope of commerical success; because it avoided so many villages passenger traffic was always limited; in the 1920s only about seventy people a week used the station at Humbie. This was not surprising considering that it sometimes took nearly an hour and a half for trains from Gifford to reach Ormiston only 16km away. Although things improved during the 1920s, it still took over 40 minutes to cover this stretch. Mineral traffic also failed to come up to expectations though the line was not a complete white elephant. It encouraged the proprietor of Wester Pencaitland to open a colliery there which employed up to 300 men and turned the settlement into a mining village.

The age of the train was soon over in this quiet rural area, for the development of motor bus sevices in the 1920s killed off passenger services within a few years. A bus service from

Edinburgh to Gifford was started in 1928 and within three years the railway had ceased to carry passengers. Freight traffic continued until 1948 when a flood carried away the bridge at Humbie. The line beyond Humbie was never reopened though the western end continued to carry some goods traffic until 1962.

Some of the mainline stations such as Drem and Dunbar still preserve much of their nineteenth-century character. Railway enthusiasts may find it interesting to look for the remains of lost stations at such places as Aberlady (470794), Gifford (529634), Gullane (488828) and Haddington (508739). The disused branch lines shown in Figure 13 also provide opportunities for exploring the East Lothian countryside by unconventional routes provided that you are prepared to divert around broken bridges. The line of the Gifford and Garvald railway passes through particularly attractive scenery.

Some Suggestions for Further Reading

Geology
   G.Y. Craig and P.M. Duff, *The Geology of the Lothians and South East Scotland: An Excursion Guide* (1975) includes some East Lothian localities. J.B. Whittow, *Geology and Scenery in Scotland* (1977) provides some background.

The Changing Landscape
   Many aspects of landscape change come out in the various Statistical Account descriptions. However, the two Board of Agriculture county reports, G. Buchan Hepburn, *General View of the Agriculture and Rural Economy of East Lothian* (1794) and R. Somerville, *General View of the Agriculture of East Lothian* (1805), survey the area at a crucial period of change.

History
   Unlike some parts of Scotland, East Lothian has not been covered by one of the multi-volume Victorian county histories which provide a mine of information on the history of, for example, Forfarshire or Peeblesshire. C.R. Green, *Haddington, or East Lothian* (1907) and J. Miller, *The Lamp of Lothian* (1844 & 1900) are about the best of the old local histories. East Lothian is, however, fortunate in having an active modern local history society. The various volumes of the *Transactions of the East Lothian Antiquarian and Field Naturalist Society* contain articles on a wide range of themes from social and economic history to architecture and the area's landed families. The *Proceedings of the Society of Antiquaries of Scotland* also contain many articles relating to the archaeology and history of East Lothian.
   Sir John Sinclair's Statistical Account of Scotland from the 1790s, and the New Statistical Account of the 1840s, contain descriptions of each parish and are a mine of information on local history as well as contemporary social and economic conditions. The East Lothian volume of the Third Statistical Account, edited by C. Snodgrass in 1953, provides a mid-twentieth century cross-section of East Lothian life and geography.

Buildings
   The most comprehensive guide is C. McWilliam & C. Wilson, *Lothian,* in the *Buildings of Scotland* series, which covers most structures from castles, churches and country houses to farmsteads and cottages – but not archaeological sites in any detail. The Royal Commission on Ancient Monuments volume on East Lothian (1924) does not cover buildings later than the seventeenth century but reviews known archaeological sites in detail, though much of this material is inevitably

dated. The Midlothian volume (1929) covers Musselburgh and district. D. MacGibbon & T. Ross, *The Castellated and Domestic Architecture of Scotland,* 5 vols. (1887-92) and *The Ecclesiastical Architecture of Scotland,* 3 vols. (1887-92) still remain standard works. For tower houses, see N. Tranter, The *Fortified House in Scotland,* Vol. 1 (1962). J.G. Dunbar, *The Architecture of Scotland* (1978) provides useful general background.

Industrial Archaeology

J. Butt, *The Industrial Archaeology of Scotland* (1967) and J. Hume, *The Industrial Archaeology of Scotland,* Vol. 1, *The Lowlands and Borders* (1976) both cover East Lothian though the range of sites which they include is rather restricted. J. Shaw, *Water Power in Scotland* (1984) makes use of some interesting East Lothian examples.

Transport

J. Thomas, *The North British Railway,* 2 vols., 1968 & 1975, provides an account of the railway era in East Lothian. For bus transport, see D.L.G. Hunter, *From SMT to Eastern Scottish* (1987).

Gazetteer of Places to Visit

This book has been designed to be read either before or after a visit to East Lothian rather than as a guidebook to be consulted on the spot. Nevertheless, for the benefit of people exploring the area by car, by cycle or on foot this gazetteer is designed to provide brief information about what to look out for in particular places. To avoid repetition of material in the text entries have been kept short with page references to the appropriate sections in the book. Two-figure National Grid references have been given to larger sites such as towns and villages, pinpointing the 1km grid square on the Ordnance Survey map in which they are located. Smaller features like castles, churches or prehistoric sites, not all of which are named on the 1:50,000 Ordnance Survey map, have been located with three-figure grid references which will pin them down to within 100 metres.

ABERLADY (4679-4680). Attractive village on south side of Aberlady Bay (nature reserve; p. 19). Formerly a burgh of barony and the port of Haddington. Old mercat cross (p. 142). Cottages in the village mainly late c18 and c19 (p. 148). Parish church has c15 tower and inside a replica of c8 cross shaft (p. 27). 1km to the east is Luffness House with remains of c16 earthwork fort (p. 75) and friary (p. 42). To the south-west are the policies of Gosford House (p. 133). To the north are remains of Kilspindie Castle (462801).

ATHELSTANEFORD (5377). Estate village laid out in later c18 by Sir David Kinloch of Gilmerton (p. 147). The village stands on a ridge and the main street runs gently downwards from the church (built 1868) and c16 doocot (p. 103) between attractive pantiled cottages (p. 147).

AULDHAME (594844). Hamlet near clifftops east of North Berwick. At 602848 are the remains of Auldhame House, a c16 tower with small cove in cliffs below.

BARNES CASTLE (529766). Also called 'The Vaults', an unfinished fortified house and courtyard from the late c16 on an unusual plan (p. 72).

BASS ROCK (603874). Accessible in summer by boat from N. Berwick. Noted for its birdlife especially gannets (p. 19). Bass Castle, scene of siege 1691-4 (p. 90), c16 chapel to St. Baldred.

BELHAVEN (6678). The original harbour of Dunbar; Belhaven is now virtually a suburb of the burgh but still retains its individuality. Belhaven Brewery (p. 185), famous for its real ales, is one of the oldest in Scotland. The south side of Belhaven Bay has some attractive coastal walks and is a venue for birdwatchers.

BLACK CASTLE (579662). Well preserved Iron Age hillfort (p. 54).

BOLTON (506701). A hamlet rather than a village. The church dates from 1809 on the site of earlier ones. Among the graves in the churchyard is that of Robert Burns' mother and brother Gilbert (p. 42). Opposite the church, a distinctive cylindrical doocot is attached to the farmstead.

BROXMOUTH (697777). Country house built in later c18 with later alterations and additions, set in attractive park.

CARBERRY HILL (374696). Scene of surrender of Mary, Queen of Scots, to the Confederate Lords, 1567 (p. 85).

CATCRAIG (718773). Small rocky creek with quarry and restored limekilns and explanatory boards. Geology trail.

CHESTERS, THE (508783). Easily accessible and impressive Iron Age fort (p. 53).

COCKENZIE AND PORT SETON (4075). Two industrial and fishing settlements which grew up around their respective harbours and have merged to form a straggling little town. Dominated by the modern power station but there are few traces of the traditional salt and pottery industries. Cockenzie House was the home of the Cadell family, enterprising merchants and industrialists (p. 200).

DIRLETON (5183-5184). One of East Lothian's most attractive villages, grouped round an extensive green (p. 140) and dominated by an imposing medieval castle (p. 62). The c17 church is offset to the north. The village contains some plain late c18 cottages and more picturesque 2-storey ones from the mid-c19. To the west are the policies of Archerfield House. The building itself, dating from the c17 and remodelled by Robert Adam, is now only a shell.

DOON HILL (685757). Remains of Dark Age timber halls marked out (p. 57). Good vantage point for Dunbar battlefield (p. 87).

DREM (510795). A small hamlet centred round the railway station. Opposite the station is an attractive group of early c19 farmworkers' cottages. The road leads past them to a large mid-c19 farmstead.

DUNBAR (680790). Medieval burgh and important harbour from c17 on, Dunbar has retained much of its old character. Full description of burgh p. 162, harbour p. 213, castle p. 59, church p. 38.

DUNBAR, BATTLEFIELD (696767). Site of battle between Scottish Covenanting forces under General Leslie and Cromwell's troops, 1650 (p. 87).

DUNGLASS (767719). Rather austere but very fine collegiate church (p. 34). Nearby at 763718 is the 'French Camp', actually an English fort from the campaigns of the late 1540s (p. 75).

EAST FORTUNE (5578). Museum of flight affiliated to the Royal Museum of Scotland. Admission free, open daily July and August plus special open days. Range of aircraft from biplanes to modern bombers.

EAST LINTON (5977). Something between a big village and a small town. At an important crossing place of the R. Tyne, with c16 bridge (p. 205). Its location on the main road through the county brought a lot of trade and prosperity in late c18-c19, reflected in the buildings in the main streets. Nearby is parish church of Prestonkirk, mainly Georgian but with very fine c13 chancel (p. 32). In the churchyard is the grave of Andrew Meikle, inventor of the threshing machine (p. 113), who worked as a millwright in this area. Also nearby is Preston Mill (see below), an accessible doocot (p. 103) and the classical facade of Phantassie farm, c.1840 (p.113).

EASTER BROOMHOUSE (680767). Large prehistoric standing stone in field next to farm (p. 26).

ELPHINSTONE (390699). Impressive c15 tower house, largely demolished due to mining subsidence (p. 70).

FALSIDE CASTLE (377710). Ruined c15 tower house with large c16 extension. Commands find view of Musselburgh and battlefield of Pinkie.

FENTON TOWER (544821). On conspicuous ridge south of North Berwick, a ruined c16 L-plan tower house.

FIDRA (513869). Island 1km offshore, NW of N. Berwick. Can be reached by boat from N. Berwick in summer. Colony of terns and other birdlife (p. 19), lighthouse, remains of medieval monastery (p. 33).

GARLETON HILLS (5076). Low but rocky range of hills north of Haddington. Geology p. 11. Features of interest include monument to Earl of Hopetoun on summit (excellent viewpoint), haematite mine, Garleton Castle, badly ruined (509768), small hillfort (508762) and Barnes Castle (q.v.).

GARVALD (5870). Irregular, attractive village hidden in steep little valley on edge of Lammermuirs. Some interesting old houses and cottages. The parish church is c19.

GIFFORD (5367-5368). An early example of a planned estate village from the end of the c17 (p. 148). Dominated by the avenue leading to Yester House. The whitewashed church and cottages give it a dazzling appearance on a sunny day.

GLADSMUIR (4573). The old parish church of 1695 is adjacent to the c19 one and there are some attractive tombstones in the churchyard.

GOSFORD HOUSE (453787). Open to the public at certain times. A magnificent country house designed by Robert Adam for the Earl of Wemyss at the end of the c18, though later remodelled (p. 133). The interior is particularly fine.

GULLANE (4882). The village was decaying in the early c17 and the parish church was moved to Dirleton (p. 32). The ruins of the medieval parish church can be seen in the centre of the village. Gullane developed as a holiday, and particularly as a golfing, centre from the mid-c19 and its still retains this character today.

HADDINGTON (5173). The head burgh and main market centre of East Lothian from medieval times. Because of limited growth in the c19 and c20, aided by sensitive post-war conservation, Haddington has retained much of its old character and is one of the best-preserved old burghs in Scotland. Full description p. 153. For traditional industries in the town, see p. 184.

HAILES CASTLE (575758). Impressive medieval curtain wall castle (p. 61). Dept. of Environment: open to public.

HUMBIE (4562). Small hamlet. The parish church, which only dates from 1800, is at 461638, away from the village and closer to Humbie House. There are some fine old tombstones in the churchyard. At Humbie itself is the Children's Village, a loose group of cottages originally built as children's holiday homes. Picturesque mill nearby on Humbie Water.

INNERWICK (720740). Small village in rather exposed setting. The parish church dates from 1784. There are some attractive c18 cottages in the village and some interesting farms nearby. At 735737 is Innerwick Castle, a badly ruined late-medieval curtain-wall castle (p. 66).

INVERESK (3472). Now a suburb of Musselburgh but the original parish centre. The church and churchyard stand within the limits of a Roman fort. The church only dates from 1805 and replaces an earlier one built largely of Roman stonework. There is an interesting group of c19 and c20 mills on the River Esk nearby (340720).

JOHN MUIR COUNTRY PARK (6478). West of Dunbar. 1667 acres on south side of Tyne estuary. Parking and nature trails. John Muir was conservationist and founder of the first National Parks in The United States.

JOHNSCLEUCH (631664). Simple 2-storey fortified house at head of Whiteadder Water. Probably c17 remodelling of earlier structure (p. 70).

KEITH (449643). The medieval parish church (p. 33) stands ruined near Keith Marischal, a c16 tower with later alterations and enlargements.

LENNOXLOVE (515720). Formerly known as Lethington, seat of Maitlands of Lethington. Massive medieval tower house with later extensions. Open to the public (p. 71).

LUFFNESS HOUSE (475805). On outskirts of Aberlady, Luffness seems superficially to be a c16 tower house with later alterations but it may hide the vestiges of a great c13 castle. Open to the public at certain times. In grounds are vestiges of a medieval friary (p. 42).

MORHAM (557726). Lost village (p. 144). Attractive little parish kirk of 1724 which requires careful map reading to find.

MUSSELBURGH (3472). Town which developed in c16 and c17 as burgh of barony. Full description p. 168. Features of interest include c16 bridge over Esk (p. 170), c16 tolbooth (p. 169), market place and Pinkie House (p. 127).

MYRETON MOTOR MUSEUM (4879). Privately owned collection of vintage cars and vehicles.

NORTH BERWICK (5585). An ancient royal burgh and fishing port which never developed beyond a village until the coming of the railway made it a fashionable resort and commuter settlement. Fragments of the old parish church can be seen on a promontory by the shore (p. 40). This was allegedly the scene of the activities of the North Berwick witches (p. 45). The town has an interesting museum of local history, archaeology and natural history. The sharp cone of North Berwick Law (p. 177) provides an outstanding view of the Firth of Forth. Fine cliff walks to east and west and views of the Bass Rock and other islands.

NUNRAW. Modern Cistercian abbey (593700), p. 45 and c16 Z-plan tower house with later additions (598707), p. 72.

OLDHAMSTOCKS (7470). Attractive village with green, mercat cross and some pretty cottages. The parish church is mainly c18 with later alterations on earlier foundations.

ORMISTON (415694). Attractive estate village laid out by John Cockburn of Ormiston in 1730s (p. 146) with older mercat cross (p. 143). Later developed as mining village (p. 150).

PENCAITLAND (4468-4469). Two separate villages, Easter and Wester, on either side of the R. Tyne. The parish church, in Easter P., is one of the most attractive in East Lothian, c16 and c17 on medieval foundations (p. 32). The churchyard has some fine c17-c18 tombstones. The mercat cross (p. 143) is in Wester P. which developed in later times as a mining village (p. 150). Both settlements have some pretty cottages. Immediately north is Winton House (p. 126).

PENKAET CASTLE (FOUNTAINHILL) (425677). Attractive late c16-c17 mansion with walled garden and doocot (p. 123).

PENSHIEL (641632). Remains of medieval grange, or farm belonging to Cistercian monks of Melrose Abbey (p. 44).

PILMUIR HOUSE (486695). Attractive c17 laird's house (p. 124).

PINKIE, BATTLEFIELD (361717). Site of Scots defeat in 1547 by English army commanded by Protector Somerset (p. 77).

PORT SETON (see COCKENZIE).

PRESTON (390740). Attractive old village centre on outskirts of Prestonpans. Magnificent mercat cross (p. 142), impressive tower house, Preston Tower (p. 73), two fine early c17 mansions, Northfield House and Hamilton House (p. 122) and two good examples of doocots (p. 103). The site of the Battle of Prestonpans lies to the east (p. 92). Bankton House (p. 128), home of Col.

Gardiner, who was killed in the battle, stands roofless and forlorn south of the station.

PRESTON MILL (595779). p. 180. National Trust for Scotland. Restored early water-powered corn mill and kiln with exhibition on milling. Guided tours.

PRESTONGRANGE (372738). p. 194. Scottish Mining Museum. Cornish beam engine is centrepiece but also colliery locomotives and other machinery remains of brick kilns, information centre and exhibitions. Open daily, admission free.

PRESTONPANS (3874). Developed as industrial burgh in c17 with coalmining and salt pans (hence name) (p. 172). Later industries included pottery and chemicals (p. 199). Interesting late c16 parish church with some good tombstones in churchyard.

PRESTONPANS, BATTLEFIELD (4074). Scene of defeat of Sir John Cope by Charles Edward Stuart's Jacobite army in 1745. Description p. 92. Parts of battlefield have not changed greatly but little to see. Monument to Colonel Gardiner, dragoon commander, killed in sight of his house of Bankton at (394739).

REDHOUSE (463770). 2km E. of Longniddry. Interesting c16 tower house extended in c17 and still preserving its enclosing barmkin and some of its outbuildings (p. 72).

SALTCOATS CASTLE (485819). Late c16 castle, largely ruined but with some interesting architectural features (p. 73).

SALTOUN (4667-4767). Like Pencaitland, two settlements, although West Saltoun is only a hamlet. East Saltoun has the parish church (early c19) and some interesting estate cottages.

SAMUELSTON (4870). Straggling hamlet with some attractive old farmsteads and houses; off the beaten track beside the R. Tyne.

SETON (418751). Magnificent c16 collegiate church (p. 34). Seton House designed by Robert Adam, 1789, in castellated style on site of late-medieval Seton Palace (p. 34).

SKATERAW (7375). A harbour was built here to allow the local limestone to be burnt using imported coal, and shipped out. (p. 212). Remains of limekilns and some traces of the original harbour works.

SPOTT (6775). Small village south of Dunbar. Spott House has a long history but was totally redesigned by Wm Burn in the 1830s with Jacobean and Tudor decoration.

STENTON (6274). Small but attractive village with tower of old c16 parish church. Reconstructed tron or weighbeam in centre of village. At the N. end of the village is the curious Rood Well, a medieval holy well (p. 37).

STONEYPATH TOWER (597714). c15 tower house in strong defensive position above steep valley (p. 69).

TANTALLON CASTLE (596851). One of Scotland's most imposing medieval castles with dramatic clifftop site. Stronghold of powerful Douglas family. Department of Environment – open to public (p. 64).

TRANENT (4072). Developed as the centre of East Lothian's coalfield from c17 onwards. Line of early c18 colliery waggonway converted to footpath (p. 215). Tower House which has been swallowed up by the expanding town is now badly ruined. Parish church, on the northern edge of the town towards Cockenzie, has very fine collection of tombstones (p. 42) and dovecote nearby. The churchyard provides a good vantage point for the battlefield of Prestonpans (p. 92).

TRAPRAIN LAW (582748). Prominent whalebacked hill south of A1 between Haddington and East Linton. Steep sides with crags for rock climbing on south. Geology p. 11. On top are extensive remains of huge hillfort and tribal capital occupied from the late Bronze Age into the post-Roman period p. 55.

TYNINGHAME (610792). Attractive c19 estate village with sawmill and pantiled cottages, factor's house, school (p. 146). Nearby is Tyninghame House (p. 131) and in grounds the remains of the old parish church with fine Norman decoration (p. 31).

WHITE CASTLE (613687). Prominent Iron Age hillfort in Lammermuirs: readily-accessible location beside minor road from Garvald to Cranshaws (p. 54).

WHITEKIRK (596815). Small village with attractive parish kirk. Medieval pilgrimage centre to holy well (p. 36). Nearby is teind barn incorporating remains of tower house (p. 36).

WHITTINGHAME (6073). Unusual that this parish does not have a village at its centre, only a handful of scattered houses. The church dates from 1820. Whittinghame Tower (602732) is a c15-16 tower house in a strong defensive position.

WINTON HOUSE (449696). Attractive Jacobean mansion (p. 126).

YESTER HOUSE (543672). The policies around the house were laid out in the later c17 and the original village of Bothans with its parish church rebuilt as Gifford (p. 148). The mansion (open to the public at certain times) replaced an earlier fortified house and dates from the early c18 though remodelled by William and Robert Adam (p. 129). Also in the grounds are the remains of the medieval Yester Castle with the famous underground Goblin Ha' (p. 66).

Index

229